250+ fundraising ideas
for your charity, society,
school and PTA

Published by Nell James Publishers
PO Box 588, Chorley, Lancashire PR6 6FZ, UK
www.nelljames.co.uk
info@nelljames.co.uk

British Library Cataloguing-in-Publication Data
A catalogue record for this book is available from the British Library.

ISBN 978-0-9567024-0-1

First published 2011

Printed in Great Britain.

250+ fundraising ideas for your charity, society, school and PTA

Practical and simple money making ideas for anyone raising funds for charities, hospices, societies, clubs and schools

Paige Robinson

NELL JAMES PUBLISHERS

Dedicated to all fundraisers
and the fantastic work you do.

Table of contents

Introduction

Having been an avid fund-raiser for my daughter's school for many years, as well as for national charities and a local children's hospice, I have frequently trawled the internet and fundraising events searching for new and fresh ideas that I could use in a forthcoming event I was planning or participating in. I must pay thanks to my family at this point who have spent many weekends attending summer fetes on the constant look out for new ideas that I could draw upon or adapt in some way. Not that they complained too much with an ice-cream in one hand and a lucky dip toy in another!

It was with this huge folder of ideas that I approached Nell James Publishers and I am delighted to work with them in putting together an affordable book for you to turn too when planning your next charity, society, club, church or school fundraising event. With over 250 ideas contained in this book, covering the sublime (a sponsored blindfold, page 11) to the ridiculous (a 'baked bean wellington race', page 16), I hope you find something new and motivating, as without your fabulous work many charities, societies and schools would not have the funds they desperately require to help improve the lives of others. Some words of advice though before you begin:

◊   When planning an event, make sure you include a wide variety of stalls and not too many of one particular type: for example, too many 'things to buy' stalls and too few 'activity' ones. So, when planning an event ensure you have sufficient games, activities, refreshments, making stalls, buying stalls and general entertainment.

◊   Think of the person likely to be attending your event. Not everybody likes the idea of a pogo stick race or alternatively scented lavender bags for their underwear drawer. Unless your event is quite specialised in terms of its theme or you are appealing to a certain demographic, it is worth remembering that your event should appeal to as wide a mix of people as possible.

◊   Always remember what you are trying to do: encourage someone to hand over their hard earned money in return for something. This 'something' could be the sense of supporting a worthwhile cause or the pleasure in taking part in an activity with others. This 'something' could also be buying something lovely to eat, drink, keep or make. So always ensure the 'something' you are offering is worth what they paid.

◊   Think of your supporters, parents or parishioners. Whilst you need them to donate money (either by buying something or taking part in an activity), you don't want to exhaust them financially. Make sure that if one person did a number of the things on offer (for example, buy a raffle ticket, have a go at a few activities and buy one drink and a portion of food), ensure that it is not too expensive and balanced with the 'free activities' on offer, such as any entertainment being put on for their enjoyment. Events should not be measured purely on how much money is raised (although this is undoubtedly important!) but consideration should also be given to whether those attending the event have a sense of 'value for money'. People consciously or unconsciously associate the experience they had with the amount of money they spent. So if you want them to return the following year or to come to your next event, remember to be good value!

◊   People like to donate when they know it is going to something specific (for example, a kidney dialysis machine for the local hospital or new library books for the school). It gives a sense of purpose to the donation and creates great publicity when the target has been reached and the item bought. Also, if it can be broken down to what a typical donation is worth, such as £5 equates to two new books or three minutes of life-saving treatment, it shows people that their contribution will make a huge difference to someone's life and that every penny and pound really does count. Even if you have a huge sum to achieve, such as £2 million every year for the running of a children's hospice, knowing that the £10 someone has donated allows a terminally ill child to spend five minutes in a wonderful sensory room suddenly makes someone's donation far more personal.

◊   A fundraising thermometer is a fantastic visual aid to encourage people to reach a goal, especially if it is a target that is to be achieved over a period of time. It can spur people on to 'break the thermometer' at the top and is a constant reminder on how far everyone has to go. Regular updates on how it is progressing with your supporters and the local press will keep your fundraising in the media spotlight as well as encourage everyone to keep working towards the target.

◊   Remember Gift Aid. If you are a registered charity, ensure you claim the UK tax that has been paid on the donation via Gift Aid (see www.hmrc.gov.uk/individuals/giving/gift-aid.htm for more information).

◊   When planning and running your fundraising event, remember to aim for the **STARS!**
S – Simple (keep events simple so it is easier to manage)
T – Trim costs (keep costs down)
A – Advertise (more publicity means more people attend)
R – Rally round (don't be shy to ask for help and volunteers)
S – Smile (because if you enjoy yourself, others will too!)

◊   And finally, probably the most important thing to remember is that whilst every event is about fundraising, never forget that it starts with the word FUN and that is exactly what your event should be!

Finally, I would like to take this opportunity to thank you for supporting my fundraising efforts, as all royalties from the sale of this book are donated to the NSPCC (National Society for the Prevention of Cruelty to Children). So thank you on behalf of the NSPCC!

If you have any suggestions or fundraising ideas that you would like to see included in a second edition of this book (with your help the next book could be titled '500+ fundraising ideas'!), then please email me via the publishers, Nell James Publishers (info@nelljames.co.uk).

Good luck with your fundraising work! It is fantastic what you are doing, and, on behalf of all the people, children, animals or environmental causes you are supporting, THANK YOU!

Paige Robinson

Sponsorship

Sponsorship is a brilliant way of raising a significant amount of money as well as creating greater awareness about your cause. All you require are enthusiastic people to take up a challenge - because any sponsoring event has to include some kind of challenge - and some sponsorship forms (see page 123 for websites that provide sample sponsorship forms that you can use as a template). Remember to include 'Gift Aid' on your sponsorship form if you are in the UK so that you can claim back the tax from the government (see page 122 for the government website about Gift Aid), and make sure you mention on the form what you are raising money for. Donors like to know that their money is going towards something specific such as new computers for the classroom or furniture for a family room in a children's hospice, so include as much information written as clearly as possible, on your form.

You can also set up an online sponsorship form via websites such as www.justgiving.com, which is an effective way of acquiring support and money from people further afield and even abroad. If you do set up an online sponsorship form, ensure you promote it as much as possible. Put the link to the form on Facebook, Twitter and any other social networking sites you are connected to. You can also add the link to the sponsorship form to the bottom of emails you send out (both personal ones and work ones if possible) and make sure you ask friends and family members to circulate the link to your form to their wide circle of friends, contacts and distant relatives. By doing all of this, you are creating a ripple effect and the more ripples you create, the more people who know about your fundraising efforts and the good cause you are trying to raise money for. Online sponsorship forms have the additional benefit of ensuring the donation is paid straight away so you don't have to spend weeks after the event chasing people for their sponsorship money.

Another idea to consider is 'matched giving'. The company that the person being sponsored works for, or a separate company who are supportive of your cause, might agree to match the amount of money raised 'like for like'. So for every pound or dollar that you raise, they then match the same amount, turning £100 raised into £200. It is worth asking your employer or any businesses that have supported your cause in the past whether they are interested in adopting a 'matched giving' scheme as it creates great publicity for them and, more importantly, raises valuable funds for you.

1. One day fast

A sponsorship idea that doesn't take too much organising and is especially effective if the charity you are supporting is associated with famine or poverty. If a one day's fast is too much, then why not skip a fortnight of 'coffee and cakes' at work and ask colleagues to donate the saved money to your charity? If you have a tuck shop at school or club, ask the children if they would be interested in a sponsored 'tuck shop fast' for a period of time, say a week, with parents and friends sponsoring them to abstain from the lures of jelly beans and crisps!

2. Quit it

Whether it is smoking or chocolate, giving up something either permanently or temporarily is a popular sponsorship idea that takes very little planning and can be combined with a theme to highlight issues linked to your charity, society or school. If your charity is linked to an illness associated with indulgences in modern life (such as obesity and heart disease or smoking and lung cancer), then a sponsored quit-it is an effective way of raising much needed awareness as well as financial support. For schools, why not do a sponsored 'quit the car' scheme, where children are encouraged to walk the last few hundred yards to school?

3. Weight loss

This works well either individually or as a group of people trying to lose a substantial total amount of weight. A group weight loss is also an effective way of losing weight as you don't want to let the others down and by giving each other support you can help each other as well as raise money. So while you lose the pounds, encourage friends and family to donate their pounds! Just make sure everyone follows a sensible diet and exercise plan and that everyone taking part in the sponsored weight loss consults their GP before starting for medical advice.

4. Sponsored silence

A great sponsorship idea for children of all ages to try, with half an hour for the little ones to manage yet a whole morning for older children to do, and it isn't just schools that can do this simple sponsorship idea but also dance clubs and sport societies working together as a team to stay silent. If run as a school fundraiser, why not tie it in with lessons on the freedom of speech and human rights, holding it on 11th February, the anniversary of the date Nelson Mandela was released from prison in 1990?

Next are some educational and brain-testing sponsorship ideas, perfect for schools and societies, or those who prefer thinking challenges:

5. Read-a-thon

If you have reluctant readers, or even enthusiastic ones, set a sponsored challenge to read as many books by on particular author or a wide variety of books in a set period of time (e.g. 24 hours, a weekend or in one school term). There could then be a literature test afterwards to make sure no-one has cheated or a reward for the child who has read the most. Another way of ensuring the books have been read properly is to ask the readers

geology challenge to learn about fossils, rocks and minerals.

11. News-a-thon

One for the adults, teachers or older pupils: challenge everyone to read a newspaper every day for a week for a current affairs test with participants being sponsored on the number of questions they answer correctly. It could be run individually or as teams (maybe a team from year six versus a team of teachers?) with the winners getting a prize or the losers having to do a forfeit.

12. Bio-a-thon

Why not sponsor budding doctors and nurses to learn all the bones in the human body (or budding vets to learn the bones of an animal) and then challenge them to put a skeleton back together again within a short time? Or challenge participants to label all the parts as quickly as possible with the fastest individual or team winning a prize or house points.

13. Chem-a-thon

For scientists and Marie Curies of the future, set a sponsorship challenge to learn the periodic table or the compounds of metals or to find the chemical breakdown of household items for a huge chemistry test.

14. Music-a-thon

Another idea is to have a sponsored music event. This can either be a sponsored music endurance challenge (for example, a team of pianists playing the piano continually for twenty-four hours, taking it turns through the day and night but the piano is continually played the whole time) or a learning challenge, where pupils are sponsored to learn about various composers and their music for a 'guess the composer' test. Alternatively, test them on the music from a particular decade, learning perhaps about rock and roll and the 1950s.

15. Puzzle-a-thon

Put together a collection of puzzles (such as Sudoku, word searches, crosswords, anagrams and cryptograms) and sponsor people to complete as many puzzles as quickly as possible or within a set time. Or have a sponsored contest of chess, draughts or backgammon (or combine all three) with participants sponsored for the number of games they play or win in a period of time, such as over one day or a weekend.

16. Sponsored blindfold

This is a fantastic sponsorship idea for schools, clubs and societies as it not only raises money but can be run as part of a lesson on disability, developing awareness and empathy to blindness and the support required. Participants are paired together, one blindfolded and the other person being their guide for one hour in the morning, swapping over in the afternoon. They could then write about their experiences and challenges. Other disabilities and the problems faced by others could be considered too. A 'sponsored one-arm' shows how hard it is to do everyday tasks when one arm is tied behind your back and a 'sponsored deafness' (with sound-proof headphones) can show how strange the world is with no sounds. It is sometimes only when we all try living the lives of others that we understand what they are dealing with and this is a great sponsorship idea to create awareness as well as raise funds.

For those who prefer physical challenges, why not try one of these sponsorship ideas?

17. Marathon

Not for the faint-hearted, this is a popular and demanding physical sponsorship idea for adults that can either be done individually or as a group. Either compete in a well established and official marathon (such as the London, New York or Sydney marathon), or measure out your own long distance between two towns or a certain number of laps of a football pitch or cricket ground. Just make sure that you consult your GP before undertaking any strenuous physical activity and that the training and preparation starts in plenty of time before the actual event. Also ensure you listen to the advice of personal trainers or experts in marathon running regarding a suitable training programme, warming-up and cooling-down adequately, consuming the right kind of energy and hydration.

18. Sponsored walk

For those who like a physical challenge yet aren't keen on a marathon, a sponsored walk is a gentler sporting idea yet still challenging, especially if the distance is quite far or you do it in fancy dress or three-legged. A sponsored walk between two landmarks or along Hadrian's Wall is popular. Alternatively, why not organise a 'Moonlight Walk', a popular event for women only who walk together in a large group and through the night, wearing their bra outside of their top (or just their bra on top)? This is a popular awareness campaign to promote breast cancer and how to check for symptoms (www.walkthewalk.org).

19. Fun run

A shorter distance than a marathon and with the emphasis being on fun, this could be a sponsored fun run around the local football pitch either on a space hopper, or on piggy back, or in fancy dress, or even three-legged. The more ridiculous it is the better! This is a popular challenge for children to participate in with their parents or for them to cheer along their rather embarrassed mum or dad!

20. Sponsored swim

This can either be a long distance sponsored swim such as the race held on Lake Windermere in the Lake District each year or a swim in the sea on a cold winter's day or a number of laps of your local swimming pool. Alternatively, you could organise a swimming relay race for children or adults to participate in with everybody cheering each other on to swim as many lengths or widths as possible. Just make sure there are enough qualified lifeguards on duty to supervise any children participating in or watching the event. If any novice swimmers are taking part, ensure they are accompanied by a competent adult swimmer and are wearing appropriate arm bands and float jackets.

21. Sponsored cycle ride

Just like the previous idea, this can either be a sponsored long distance cycle ride, a circuit challenge or part of a fun bike ride (using old BMX bikes, tricycles, unicycles or tandem bicycles). You could even use an exercise bike and complete a sponsored 'UK cycle-a thon', with participants cycling so many miles each, all day and all night, until the total distance cycled is the length of the country, from John O' Groats in Scotland to Lands End in Cornwall.

22. Three Peaks Challenge / hiking

Following on from the marathon and walking challenges, why not try a sponsored hiking challenge or more specifically, the Three Peaks Challenge, where people climb Ben Nevis in Scotland, Scar Fell in the Lakes and Snowdonia in North Wales, all in one weekend? Not for the faint-hearted! If this is a bit too much, you could always organize a sponsored hike or climb up just one of these mountains.

23. Triathlon

If one of the above events wasn't enough, how about combining running, cycling and swimming and doing one gruelling spon-sored event? You could even stage a children's triathlon with a running, cycling and skipping (instead of swimming) challenge. Alternatively combine three ball related sports to create a 'ball-triathlon', such as dribbling a football in between cones, then

doctor before starting any training or physical exertion for medical advice, especially if you have a medical condition relating to your blood pressure or heart, and of course acquire full training from suitably qualified professionals. Check the credentials and references of your fully qualified instructor and only use a highly reputable company. You may also want to check your own insurance as well to ensure you are covered for any personal accidents or cancellations. And good luck! Whilst I would never throw myself out of plane I applaud those who do for the sake of raising money for their charity.

Finally, let us not forget all the unusual, silly, bizarre and quite simply rather insane sponsorship ideas that are popular with participators, sponsors and spectators:

31. Hair ideas
So many ways you can gather sponsorship money from your hair. Grow it (a beard or a moustache), shave it (a beard, moustache, eyebrows even or a full head of hair!), dye it a bright colour for a whole week or even wax it (preferably the legs or chest hair of men!) If you are thinking of doing something quite daring with your hair anyway - whether to have it cut from waist length to shoulder, or are considering shaving off a moustache you have had for years - don't miss the opportunity to raise money for your charity or school by being sponsored to do something you were going to do anyway.

32. Baked beans challenges
I'm not quite sure when baked beans became such a popular part of sponsorship challenges, but I have seen a number of 'baked bean' related ideas over the years. If everyone in your charity, society, club or school donated one tin of baked beans, there are a number of sponsorship activities that you can run at very little cost or organization. Ideas include: sitting in a bath full of beans the longest, or a 'baked beans in your welly' race, or how about

the number of baked beans you can eat in one minute with a tooth-pick or chopsticks!

33. Sit in / eating challenges

Following from the previous idea, there are numerous other sit-in sponsorship ideas that you could do - a bath full of custard, a paddling pool of ice, a foot bath of jelly. You MUST hold the sponsored 'sit-in' at a public place so that people walking by can throw any loose change into a bucket. Make sure you have signs saying why the person is sitting in a paddling pool of custard and what they raising money for! Additional eating challenges are: how many dry crackers can you eat in one minute, how many hotdogs in one minute, or how many weetabix (or dry shredded wheat) can you eat in one minute?

34. Bed / Car / Bus / Truck push

If it has four wheels and is quite heavy then why not get a team together and push it for charity? This can be a 'push' around your local football ground or even through your town or village as long as the council and police allow it! A sponsored 'push' creates a strong visual fundraising activity that generates a great deal of local publicity and it goes without saying that everyone pushing the bed/car/bus/truck are in fancy dress! If it is an old bed on coasters that you are pushing, then dress in old pyjamas, dressing gowns and slippers with your hair in a net and rollers. If it is an old bus you are pushing, then why not dress up from the 1960s and re-enact Cliff Richard's *Summer Holiday*? You could have the music playing out too! Just make sure you have enough volunteers to push the object so no-one hurts themselves, and that someone responsible is in charge of steering!

35. Pyramid of cards

This is a good sponsorship idea for adults with a steady hand and not a nervous disposition as a great deal of calmness and patience is required. Participators are sponsored to build the tallest pyramid of cards, with the winner of the highest tower winning a prize. This event creates a great photo opportunity for your local newspaper, which ensures more people learn about your fundraising efforts.

36. Sponsored knit

The longest scarf? The biggest jumper? The most baby bonnets knitted in a weekend? All of these are great knitting sponsorship ideas and all the knitted items can then be sold or auctioned afterwards - so two fundraising ideas from just some knitting needles and balls of wool. Alternatively, people who can sew can be sponsored to create a huge patchwork quilt, which again can be sold or auctioned after the event. Each square could mean something about the charity, society, school or club you are raising money for, or just contain all the names of the children at the school or children's hospice who have helped to make the patchwork blanket.

37. Guinness book of records

Have a look in the *Guinness Book of Records* for a challenge you think you can beat or at least have a go at. It would certainly get into your local paper and would be great publicity for your cause, as well as making everyone involved a *Guinness Book of Record* holder!

Raffles and lotteries

Raffles and lotteries are popular and successful sources of fundraising income for many charities, schools, clubs and societies and you can never underestimate the fun in winning a good prize for just fifty pence on a bottle tombola at a Summer fair! It can, however, be difficult to acquire good prizes. Ask parents or businesses associated with your school, club or society to donate prizes or contact local companies directly to see if they can donate something in exchange for publicity at the event. You can also ask supporters to donate one small value item, such as a jar of jam, a packet of tea or biscuits, and then make up a variety of food hampers using the donations. Consider services as well as actual items, such as a free one hour dance class, a car valet, a children's haircut, a home manicure. If you don't have many prizes, consider a 'raffle of odd-jobs' from your supporters such as an hour's ironing, an afternoon of gardening or a home-cooked dinner as a prize.

38. Raffle tickets (sold on the day)

Selling tickets on the day is the easiest way of holding a raffle and doesn't require any special tickets to be printed. However, you will need some confident and outgoing people to sell the tickets and not to hide behind a table - they also need to be walking among the crowds encouraging people to buy. Also some of the tickets should be folded before the event begins as folding hundreds of tickets can sometimes be the most time consuming part of a raffle. The prizes for the raffle should be prominently displayed and make sure the time of the draw is well advertised so that everyone knows how long they should stay for the exciting draw. If local companies have donated prizes make sure that their names and prizes are well publicized as agreed and it is always polite to send a thank you letter after the event with an update on how well the raffle went. This shows that you haven't taken their donation for granted and encourages them to support your cause again in the future. Finally, you need someone with a loud voice or a microphone to shout out the winning tickets and prizes and someone to pull out the winning tickets. Good luck!

39. Raffle tickets (sold in advance)

Whilst selling raffle tickets on the day is an easy and effective way of holding a raffle, you undoubtedly raise more money by selling tickets in advance. It requires far more work and organization, as well as some impressive prizes to promote on the specially printed tickets, yet selling in advance does allow tickets to be sold to people not attending the event and therefore reaching a wider circle of family, friends, colleagues and distant supporters. To sell tickets in advance you need to apply for a licence from your local council and for someone to act as the promoter. You will also require specially printed raffle tickets and at least three top prizes to mention on the tickets. Whilst it is harder to organize, more money is usually raised this way despite the additional cost of printing the tickets. You could even have a prize for the person who sells the most tickets!

40. Tombola

I love a tombola! Bottle tombola, chocolate tombola, cake tombola, bits-and-bobs tombola, even a jam and chutney tombola or how about a 'flowers and plant pot' tombola! So much fun to be had for just one pound and three raffle tickets pulled from a tombola or a box! You do require quite a lot of prizes to fill a table though, but if you asked all your club or society members, church congregation or school children to bring in one item such as chocolate, then you will soon have a packed table of chocolate boxes, bars of chocolate, Easter eggs and other chocolate delights. You could even combine it with another activity to raise prizes - how about a non-school uniform day in return for one bar of chocolate bought in? You will also need raffle tickets to label the prizes, which should be done in advance of the event. To make it easy for you and the person playing the game to find any winning prizes, just use the 'fives' and 'zero' raffle tickets as the winning numbers. Fold all the other numbers too as you will need some non-winning tickets inside the tombola to make the game more of a challenge and to encourage people to keep spending money and trying their luck.

41. Lottery bonus ball

This fundraising idea can be run as a one-off event or as an ongoing fundraiser throughout the year, where supporters pay a pound per bonus ball draw by direct debit, so two pounds a week if following the UK National Lottery draws on Wednesday and Saturday. This is how it works: for £1 supporters choose a number from the numbers drawn (so 1 to 49 for the UK National Lottery). Whoever chooses the number drawn as the bonus ball wins £30. If all 49 numbers are taken and £30 is paid out to the winner, the school, society, club or charity receives £19 per draw, and with two draws a week this brings in just under £2,000 a year. Alternatively, if this is too difficult to run or you do not have enough members who would like to regularly donate in this way, then why not hold a one-off lottery bonus ball? Or have your own selection of numbered balls (maybe using table tennis balls and a marker pen) - if you charge £1 per ball and have 200 balls, paying out £20 to the winner of the ball pulled out first and then two second place prizes of £10, you will still raise £160 if you 'sell' all the balls. One final note, you will require a lottery license which can be obtained from the licensing department at your local Council due to the Gambling Act of 2005. This currently costs £40 for the first year and £20 thereafter.

42. Weather lottery

Similar to the previous fundraising idea, this is a lottery system that is based on the weather and temperatures of various destinations in the world, as recorded by the UK newspaper, the *Daily Mail*. Each player chooses six numbers from zero to nine and this is then matched to the second digit of Fahrenheit temperatures

21

from a selection of destinations around the world, creating a unique winning number. The person with the winning combination wins a cash prize and the associated charity receives a percentage of the donated money. There is also a 'lightning lottery' in operation, which actually gives your charity a higher percentage of the money donated. For more information and for application forms see www.theweatherlottery.com. Finally, just like the lottery bonus ball fundraising idea, you will require a lottery license from the licensing department at your local Council.

Collections

Simple yet effective, never underestimate the power of just asking people for any loose change they have in their pockets and for cash donations. Collecting spare change can also be used as part of a fun activity or challenge and is a great way of boosting your fundraising fund.

43. Collection boxes / buckets

Sometimes you just have to ask to receive or in this case provide the opportunity for people to donate. By putting collection boxes (or even empty margarine tubs with a little sticker saying 'thank you for your donated loose change') on each of the stalls at your Summer Fair, people can kindly put any spare coins they have into the boxes available. Just imagine if everyone attending your event donated 50p of loose change: 200 people doing this would bring in an extra £100 – money that would have remained in their pockets if you hadn't given them the opportunity or the idea to donate it to your good cause.

44. A mile of money

Send out a plea to your society, club or charity supporters, or the parents of your school children to collect as many coins as possible or to collect a particular coin (such as 1ps, 10ps or 20ps) in order to create a 'mile of money'. When you have collected lots and lots of coins, set a challenge to line them along the ground in the school playground or along an athletics track or in your local park to create a 'mile of money'. A mile of 1ps adds up to about £800, so imagine how much a mile of 10ps or 20ps would create or even a mile of mixed change! The coverage in your local newspaper along with some good photos would mean great publicity for your charity, society, school or good cause and you never know, you may actually have enough coins to create more than one mile of money!

45. Fill a bottle

Similar to the previous fundraising idea, but instead of lining all the coins around the ground, this idea is about filling something big with coins. Ask for a huge empty glass bottle from your local public house and ask people to either fill it with loose change or one particular coin, such as 5ps. You can then hold a competition to guess the amount of money in the bottle or to guess the weight of the bottle and coins or even the number of coins. Why not run all three challenges? The person closest to the actual amount (without going over!) wins a prize.

46. Build a tower

Ask people to donate a certain coin (such as 20p coins) - or use the coins collected from either of the two previous fundraising ideas - and challenge people to build the tallest tower of coins without it falling over. The person who builds the tallest single tower of coins (without using any glue!) wins a prize. A great challenge for children to have a go at or adults with a steady hand. Be careful though - parents have been known to get a little bit competitive over this challenge!

47. A smarties tube of 20ps

Buy a packet of smarties for every pupil in your school, society or club. Once they have eaten and enjoyed all the smarties, they then ask relatives and friends for their spare 20p pieces that they fill the empty smarties tube with. A full smarties tube of 20p coins will bring in £12. Multiply this by the number of children in your school, say 150, and you can raise £1,800 (minus the cost of the smarties). An enjoyable activity that could be run over half a school term, so the children have plenty of time to collect any spare 20p coins. You could even give a prize to the pupil who fills the most smarties tubes, although it might best if the prize wasn't more chocolate! How about a copy of Roald Dahl's popular children book, *Charlie and the Chocolate Factory*?

48. Legacies in will

People don't like to discuss issues of money and death, but if you are a registered charity or hospice then make sure you mention on your website how people can remember your charity in their will. It is not as difficult as people think to arrange and gives supporters the knowledge that they are still able to help others and the causes they care about even when they pass away (see www.willaid.org.uk for more information).

However, it isn't just money collections that you can encourage. There are many items you can collect for free and then sell on to people either attending your event or to an external company for a profit. Either way, the following ideas don't cost anything to run – only time and effort in acquiring donations and then selling onwards.

49. Secret presents (gifts)

If your fundraising is for a school or a club, ask parents to donate a small present suitable for an adult. Children then pay a small amount to enter a secret room without their parents and choose one of the donated gifts for their Mum or Dad, for either a Christmas, Mother's Day or Father's Day present. They then wrap and label it during the event and give it to the person on the special day. This is one of the most popular activities at our school's Christmas Fair (where we call it 'Secret Santa'), giving children independence to choose a secret present for their parents.

50. Old mobile phones

People often have old mobile phones around the house that are no longer being used and just gathering dust at the back of a drawer. Ask your supporters to donate any unused phones to your charity or school who can then sell them to a company who specialize in mobile phone recycling. Not only does it raise money for your good cause but it also has fantastic environmental benefits (www.recycle4charity.co.uk). If you can get your local newspaper behind the scheme, they could put out a plea to the wider community for unused phones to be sent your way.

51. Old clothing

Ask for old clothes and accessories to be donated and either sell them at an event such as a jumble sale or as part of a fashion evening. Alternatively, sell the items online on EBay or to a company who buy clothing, bedding and material by the weight. If you have a lot of a certain kind of clothing (such as baby clothes), then why not hold a 'baby evening' for expectant mothers run in partnership with your local mother and toddler groups? Or if you have lots of one type of accessory such as handbags, then why not hold a 'handbag swap' evening? People bring an old handbag they no longer wish to keep to the event and swap it for another they prefer, plus make a small donation to your cause. You could even raise more money by selling refreshments.

52. Ink cartridges

Old and used ink cartridges can be sent to various companies (www.cashforcartridges.co.uk or www.recycle4charity.co.uk) in exchange for money. Ask office blocks, local companies and even the council to be part of your charity or school recycling scheme by donating old cartridges to your cause. Not only does this have great environmental benefits, it also widens your group of supporters and ensures you receive a high volume of ink cartridges that raise valuable funds for your charity, club or school. As with other fundraising ideas, if you can get your local newspaper supporting your recycling scheme, then they could put out a plea to their readers to send old ink cartridges your way. Before you start asking for old and used ink cartridges, check with the companies involved the type of items they are interested in and the ones they wouldn't be able to buy. The last thing you want is lots of old ink cartridges that nobody wants to buy or recycle!

53. Stamps

Ask supporters and local businesses to collect old and used British and overseas stamps. It really doesn't matter if they have been used or are every day first or second class stamps. Used stamps can be sold by their weight and size to an independent collector or stamp collecting organisation, although contact them first to see how much they give per kilogram and that they are interested in your collection. You might even come across a rare or unusual stamp, which would give a great boost to your fundraising!

54. Foreign currency

After the summer holidays of your charity supporters, society members or school children, why not ask them for any foreign coins they have left over? Get a big jar and put it somewhere visible for people to top up with their Euros, cents and dollars. Once the jar is full, send it to a specialist company for cash such as www.cash4coins.co.uk (who at the time of writing offer a 10% discount of their charges for good causes and will collect the coins if heavy) and await a cheque for your efforts!

55. Gold

Ask for any unwanted gold (jewellery, pens, charms etc.) that can be sold to an independent dealer or company. It is best to not go through one of the many companies advertising on the television as they are often proved to not offer the best gold rates. Once you have collected gold jewellery from your supporters, find out on the internet what the value of gold is at the time you are thinking of selling. With this knowledge, visit an independent gold purchaser in person for a better rate rather than send through the post. If you do decide to go to one of the companies that ask for gold via the post then don't accept their first or even second offer - haggle for a better rate!

56. Aluminium cans

Collect aluminium cans and then sell them to a recycling agency (www.alupro.org.uk/cash-for-your-cans.html). Either focus on your group and team of supporters or ask the newspaper to get behind your appeal and ask for donations from the community. You could also ask local bars, hotels, fast food outlets, colleges, youth centres, cafes and supermarkets to help with your recycling efforts by donating empty cans to your cause. A great way to check if the can is aluminium is with a magnet - if it doesn't stick then it is the right metal.

57. Scrap metal

There are many scrap metal companies across the country who will gladly buy any scrap metal you have collected. Contact them in advance to see what kind of metal they are currently looking for and then do an appeal among your supporters and local community. Contact builders, building contractors, surveyors, renovation and demolition companies to see if they are willing to donate any scrap metal they have come across in the course of their work to your cause.

58. Used batteries

Send out an appeal to collect used batteries that can be recycled and turned into cash. Once collected send them to a specialist recycling company (www.recyclingforcash.co.uk) but make sure you collect the right batteries first, as you don't want to be stuck with lots of batteries that you can't do anything with.

59. Books

Ask for pre-loved and second-hand books to be donated by parents or supporters to your school, society, club, church or charity. These can then be sold online via Amazon Marketplace (where you list the book by ISBN as well as its condition, setting your own price for the book) or you can sell the books on a book stall at your local event. If you have a vast number of books in one genre (such as romance novels) then why not sell them as part of a themed event, such as Valentine's Day? If you end up collecting too many books, then contact your local second-hand books seller who might be interested in buying the books for a reduced price.

60. CDs, DVDs and computer games

It is amazing what can be collected and then sold on to a specialist company. Music Magpie are a company that buy old CDs, DVDs and computer games and don't charge postage costs (www.musicmagpie.co.uk). They even pay for an insured carrier service to collect the items if there are over 100. Music Magpie are use to dealing with charities and schools and even have downloadable posters and flyers for you to send out to your members. So as supporters and parents declutter their shelves by sending you their unwanted CDs, DVDs and games to you, you raise more money for your good cause!

61. Nearly new sales

Ask for toys, household goods and anything else to sell at 'Nearly new' sales. If you have many items donated of a particular kind, why not have a number of themed 'nearly new' sales throughout the year, such as a baby, children, garden or home sale? Make sure you adequately promote the sale to the wider public and not just your supporters or members as it is important to attract a strong crowd of bargain hunters! Ideally, it is best to hold the nearly new sale in a public place, or near a main road, where it will catch the attention of many people passing by.

62. Car boots and EBay

This section has given a variety of ideas on what to collect and the different companies you can sell them too. There are still two popular places to sell any items collected through donation: car boot sales and on EBay. Both have pros and cons (sometimes a great deal of effort for very little return), but make sure you advertise clearly that all money received is going to a good cause. It may stop people haggling about the price!

Games and activities

The games and activities you put on for people's enjoyment are an important part of any fundraising event, raising a considerable sum for your cause as well as lots of smiles, laughter and memories of a great day. Remember that the more fun a game or activity is, the more times people will have a go at it and that they will then tell friends or relatives to have a go too. Some activities don't require any or very little organizing; some require substantial planning. Some can be tied to other events or a theme whilst others can be run during a normal day at the office or school, showing that all you need is some willing participants and a little imagination!

63. Dressing-up or down / no school uniform:

For just £1 (or more) colleagues can come to work in fancy dress, wear their jeans, a loud tie, a Hawaiian shirt, their pyjamas, have odd shoes or odd socks, or even an 'inside-out' day with clothes back to front or inside out or both – so many possibilities! Pupils can do the same, wear all one colour or just wear 'no school uniform' for the entire day for a small charge.

64. Bad hair / hat day

This time it is all about your hair! How about a bad hair day with clips, slides, hair bands, bobbles, ribbons, hairspray, gel, glitter, styling wax and even temporary hair dye? If this is too drastic, how about 'wear a wig day'? You can even have a 'no hair day' by making everyone wear a swim hat or hair nets! Alternatively, have a 'Mad Hatter's Day' with a range of interesting hats being worn – berets, hard hats, top hats, straw hats, cowboy hats, flat caps, baseball caps, woolly hats – this is an easy way for a group of people to raise money either by donating for the pleasure of looking ridiculous or gathering support through sponsorship.

65. Pyjamas and book for bedtime

This is a popular fundraising activity for primary schools to consider on World Book Day, as well as clubs and societies that have a lot of young children as members. For a small donation, pupils come to school or their club wearing their pyjamas, dressing-gown and slippers, bringing along their favourite book and teddy bear (a good event for Foundation and Key Stage 1 pupils). You can then spend a morning or afternoon reading all the magical stories, discuss why they like the stories and then have a teddy bears' picnic with sandwiches, cake and juice! You could even relate it to a famous teddy bear such as Paddington Bear and have marmalade sandwiches!

66. Balloon release

This is a lovely fundraising activity that has a very strong visual impact. Everyone buys a numbered inflated balloon that already has a tag attached to it that says something like '*Charity Balloon Race: whoever finds this balloon, please email the number of this balloon and where you are to this email address (email address). Thank you for your help and support*'. All the bought balloons are then released into the sky and whose ever balloon travels the furthest by a certain cut-off date wins a prize. (A record of who bought which balloon is kept secure so you know whose balloon is the winner.) If you are concerned about the environmental implications of releasing lots of balloons, then you can purchase bio-degradable balloons from Fair Deal Trading (www.fairdealtrading.com).

67. Balloons in a car

All you need is a car, lots of balloons and a lot of puff! Fill a car with lots of inflated balloons (make sure you count the number of balloons going in, including the boot, and don't leave any windows open), then challenge people to guess how many balloons there are. This is a strong visual fundraising activity that doesn't actually take much planning, just effort in blowing up all the balloons. However, it is worth the effort as a car full of brightly coloured balloons can draw a great crowd at an event. If all the balloons are numbered and tagged beforehand too, then you could sell the numbers, open the doors and turns the activity into the previous fundraising idea of a balloon release race. Alternatively this game can be linked to the following fundraising idea …

68. Golden ticket balloon

Inside one of the balloons you have put in the car is a golden ticket. At the end of the event, when the number of balloons has been correctly guessed, why not ask everyone to buy a balloon for popping and if they find a golden ticket inside they win a cash prize? The balloons don't have to be in a car by the way! It is just ideal to have them in a contained space for a strong visual impact and you want to sell them all the balloons at the same time – maybe hand them out to a line of children – so that the golden ticket is found after all the balloons have been sold. Be aware though that some children (and adults!) do not like the sound of popping balloons so put up a warning sign telling people that it will get noisy!

69. Golden envelope

Carrying on with the golden ticket theme, this is a simple yet effective fundraising activity where all you need is a pack of envelopes, a pen and a golden ticket. A golden ticket is placed inside one of the envelopes, which are then sealed and placed on a table. Everyone buys a sealed ticket by writing their name on the envelope – they aren't allowed to feel the envelopes before choosing or holding them up to the light to look inside! When all the envelopes have been sold, the envelopes are opened and the person who chose the one with the golden ticket inside wins a cash prize. Simple but fun!

70. Find the Queen of Hearts

Similar to the previous idea, a deck of playing cards are laid out on a table, facing downwards. People purchase a card for £1 by writing their name and telephone number on the back. When all 52 cards are 'sold', the cards are turned over and the Queen of Hearts is revealed. Whoever wrote their name on the back of this card wins £10. A simple fundraising idea that raises £42 minus the cost of a pack of cards and you can always raise more money by having more than one pack of cards on the table. However, make sure you take out the other Queen of Hearts so there is only one winner, although you could have smaller prizes for the King, Knave and Ace of Hearts).

71. Guess the baby photo

Ask the teachers of your school to bring in a photo of themselves as a baby and run a competition to guess which baby photo belongs to which teacher. Charge an amount to enter and have a small value present as a prize. You could even do a 'Guess the Mother' competition for Mother's Day, with the pupils of your school guessing which photo is the mother of which teacher. With this kind of competition there can be lots of winners (as previous winners tell their friends the answers!) – so best to offer a small prize to the winners such as a sweet or a good prize to the first correct answer per class. The fun in this activity is not the prize necessarily but the taking part.

72. Guess the pet competition

Just like the previous fundraising idea, but this time the pupils or members of your society, club or congregation are guessing which pet belongs to which person.

73. Wet sponge

This fundraising idea is best suited to a summer day event. All you need are a few willing people (because it is a bit unfair for it to be just one person the whole time and they will probably want a break after a while!), a chair, a few buckets of lukewarm water and some big sponges. Basically, the object of the game is to pay £1 and throw three sponges at a parent, teacher or willing volunteer! Make sure the person on the chair isn't too close – there has to be a bit of a challenge to the game – and the person having the sponges thrown at them might prefer if it is just children throwing the sponges!

74. Buy a brick

If you are fundraising to raise money to build a new community hall or extension, then why not break down the costs of the build and ask people to 'buy a brick'? This is a great way to involve the community as everyone knows that they really did 'buy a brick' for the project. You could even have the names of people who donated over a certain amount chiselled into some of the bricks and then use the named bricks to build an outside wall as a constant reminder of people's generous donations.

75. Banned word box

A great fundraising idea for the office is a swear box, but why not make it harder and choose a word that is common in your organization? Why not ban the word 'no' for a whole day? Or the word 'Christmas' for the whole of December? For schools, clubs and societies, why not run a sponsored 'no negative words weekend', so pupils are sponsored by friends and family to only say positive things the whole weekend – so 'no', 'can't', 'don't want too' or 'won't' cannot be said? Great if parents want to get bedrooms tidied and vegetables eaten!

76. Hook a duck

A popular fundraising idea at summer fairs and all you need are a paddling pool full of water, lots of light floating plastic ducks (or an alternative light, floating objects such as table tennis balls?), a fishing rod, a marker pen to draw a star under some of ducks, magnets and some prizes. It might seem like a lot of items for a game, but once you have got everything you can use them again and again at future events. Float the plastic ducks (or alternative floating item) on the paddling pool, each with a magnet securely attached to the top of its head. Using the fishing rod with a magnet tied to the end, contestants pay a small charge to 'hook' a duck. If it has a star underneath, they win a prize. Alternatively, this game could be a time challenge – to 'hook' as many ducks in thirty seconds, with 1-5 ducks winning a few sweets, 6-10 ducks winning a higher value prize and 11+ ducks winning a star prize. Don't make it too easy though! If it is quite easy to get lots of ducks in thirty seconds then increase the number of ducks required for winning a prize accordingly.

77. Duck race

This is another fundraising game that uses the plastic ducks from the previous idea (or alternative floating object such as table tennis balls). Everyone chooses a plastic duck and writes their name on its collar or tag (or the duck can have a number already written on it that matches a raffle ticket that has been sold). All the ducks are then released at the top of a stream. The first duck to travel downstream, pass a finishing line wins a prize. Please be very careful with this game though as it can be dangerous for young children to play around water. Ensure the banks of the stream are safe and that all children are supervised by a responsible adult.

78. Pooh-sticks

A more environmental friendly version of the above activity is for everyone to 'buy' a numbered stick (the number correlating to the name of the person who bought the stick or a raffle ticket that has been pulled from a box or hat). The sticks are then thrown from a bridge and the first pass the winning line wins a prize. Once again, take great care at this event to ensure all children supervised and are kept well away from the water's edge as well as on the bridge.

79. Dart game

All you need is a dart board and some darts (you can buy a child-friendly magnetic dart set if young children are participating) and a box of numbers or raffle tickets from 1 to 180. The person taking part pulls a number or folded raffle ticket out of the box and has to hit that number on the dart board with three darts – not as easy as it sounds so the prize should be something worthwhile! Or, make it simpler and aim for the bullseye to win a smaller prize! Children could be asked to hit an odd or an even number.

80. Computer game night

Organise a computer game night using a sports tournament game on the Wii. Challengers pay a fee to take part in a knockout contest of a variety of sports and, after a series of contests, the overall winner receives a good prize. Money can be raised from selling food and drinks to spectators cheering the contestants on as well as organizing other games on the night such as a raffle. Alternatively, set up a computer game during a fair and have one game loaded on. Everyone, including children, are invited to play one short level of the game (so one computer whizz-kid child doesn't play it continuously for five hours!) and all the scores are recorded. The person who gets the most points, or completes the level the quickest, wins a prize (which could be donated by your local computer game shop).

81. Guess the name

A simple fundraising idea for youngsters to enjoy that only requires a teddy or doll (preferably donated by a local toy shop) and a big piece of paper or card. Once you have your donated teddy or doll, draw lots of squares on the big piece of paper and write a different first name in each of the squares. Try to choose unusual names or even names associated with your event (so 'Holly', 'Ivy', Snowflake' etc for a Christmas Fair). Choose one of the names as the correct name before the game starts and put it in a sealed envelope so no-one knows what it is. Everyone then pays a small amount to choose the name they think matches the teddy or doll, writing their name and phone number (or class number) next to their chosen name. When all the names have been picked, the winner is then revealed, who wins the donated teddy or doll as a prize.

82. Find the lollipop stick or cork

Collect (maybe through donations with your school pupils, society members, charity supporters or congregation) lots of clean bottle corks or lollipop sticks and decorate the bottom tip of half of them with a marker pen. (The decorating doesn't have to be fancy! Just a star using a silver marker pen looks good!) Next, stick all the plain and decorated lollipop sticks or corks into a tray of sand, ensuring none of the decoration can be seen. People then pay a small charge, say fifty pence, to pull three lollipop sticks or corks out of the sand. If they pull out a decorated one, they win a small prize, such as a little bag of sweets. The pulled out lollipops or corks are then popped back into the sand for someone else to have a go. (A handy tip is to get a towel draped over the tray and your hands when you put the lollipops or corks back in, so that no-one can guess where they have been placed! It is also good to move the lollipops or corks around a bit so there is no cheating!)

83. Guess the weight

This is a simple fundraising idea where all you require is something heavy for people guess its weight. The person closest (but not over!) wins a cash prize or the item being guessed (such as a huge, homemade Christmas cake, a pile of encyclopaedias donated by a local bookstore or a wheelbarrow of plants donated by a local garden centre). Alternatively, why not tie this game with a loose change donation activity ran prior to the event with everyone donating any spare coins they have? The total weight of all the coins is then guessed during the event as well as the amount of money collected.

84. How many in a jar

Following on from the previous idea, this time you are guessing the number of items in a jar. It can be anything from marbles, buttons, pencils, rubber bands, erasers, sweets, nuts and bolts and screws – anything as long as there are lots of them, they are not difficult to count and won't break or get crushed by being squashed into a jar (which is why I don't recommend you use cereal!) They should also be easy and cheap to collect (preferably free – how about acorns during the autumn? – as well as easy to fill a jar or big bottle with. The person who guesses the number in the jar correctly or the closest (without going over) wins a prize. Or if it is a jar of sweets, they could win the sweets!

85. Guess the length of string

Similar to above, but far easier in terms of organizing as all you need is a very long piece of string or ribbon. Using glue, stick the string or ribbon to a piece of card, winding it all over the piece of card to make it difficult to guess its length. Just make sure you measure it before you stick it down! The person who guesses the correct length of the ribbon or string in millimetres (without going over) wins a prize.

86. Face painting

Another easy and popular fundraising activity is for someone to offer face painting for a donation. As painting a full face can take a long time (with children and parents spending most of their time queuing up rather than enjoying other activities), why not charge a smaller fee for a just a few butterflies, hearts or footballs on a child's (or adult's) cheek?

87. Nail painting

For a small donation, paint the fingernails or toenails of little princesses in a glittering pink varnish or decorate their nails with fancy nail stickers. If you are a professional manicurist, why not offer your services at a fundraising event, with a percentage of all profits going to the cause you are supporting? Not only are you raising money for charity or your child's school but you are promoting your business to more people making it a great advertising opportunity, especially if you can get the local press to cover the story too. Make sure you have lots of business cards printed!

88. Hair braiding or styling

If you are good with hair, why not offer a small charge for some lovely braids, plaits, ribbons or beads in people's hair? As mentioned in the previous fundraising idea, if you are a professional hairdresser, why not offer a discount code to anyone associated with the charity or school you are supporting? Alternatively, offer to style (not wash or cut) hair at a fundraising event, with all donations going to the charity, society or school, thus promoting your business as well as raising money for a good cause.

89. Treasure hunt / Orienteering

A great activity to keep people (especially children) amused for a while is a treasure hunt, although it does take quite a bit of organization as you need to write good clues yet don't want the hidden items found prior to the hunt beginning! Hide the hunted objects - flags /Easter eggs / teddies – around the playing fields or a building and either write clues as to where people can find them or just send them out without clues but just a piece of paper for them to write down where they all are. You can either give a small value prize to everyone that wins (such as a chocolate coin to represent treasure) or a high value prize to the person or team who completes it the quickest. If running the game as a time challenge, you might want to send teams out separately as you don't want them following each other but for them to work out the clues themselves. An adult version of this is to run it as an orienteering challenge with a compass and Ordnance Survey maps. However, this ideas isn't restricted to the country-side and climbing over fences and jumping over streams! Why not challenge people to guess a series of urban landmarks from a set of clues! People pay a fee to participate (with the lure of a good prize to the winner!) and you could set the challenge over a weekend, with people having to research answers on the internet or drive around the town or city to figure out the answers!

90. Skittles

A simple fundraising idea that can be used again and again as once you have the skittles you can bring them out at future events. Mark out a level area in a hall or outside and line-up 12 skittles at the end and charge a small amount to have a go at knocking them all down with just three (or fewer!) balls. The people who knock all 12 down win a prize. Don't make it too easy though – ensure people stand far enough away with fouls for anyone crossing the line! You could also have two skittle events running – a hard one for adults and an easier one for young children!

91. Tin can alley

As above but instead of skittles on the ground being knocked over, arrange 12 empty cans on a wall on top of each other like a pyramid. For a small donation, people then throw three balls to try and knock them all off. Anyone that manages it (and don't make it too easy!) wins a prize.

92. Coconut shy

If you have the resources, invest in a coconut shy, which is basically a colourful stand that holds coconuts high up on stills. People then have to knock three coconuts off with just three balls. The only drawback with this is that the coconuts can break if the balls are thrown hard (which they will be!) so you will need quite a few replacement coconuts just in case. However, a red and white or brightly coloured coconut shy has a great visual impact at a fair, reminding people of summer days and trips to the seaside!

93. Bean bag in a bucket

Another simple and popular fundraising activity is to have ten buckets at varying distances apart and ten bean bags. The object of the game is to throw a bean bag in each of the buckets. Sounds simple but it only takes one bad throw and the game is over. Anyone who gets a bean bag in each of the buckets wins a prize. Alternatively, put numbers on each of the buckets and if the thrower gets over 50 points, they win a prize. Don't make it too easy though!

94. Bean bag ladder

Similar to the previous fundraising idea, but instead of throwing bean bags into buckets, you have to throw them in between the rungs of a ladder lying on the ground. Whoever manages to throw a bean bag in each of the rungs wins a prize! But one wrong throw and the contest is over, so not as easy as it sounds! If you lie a long, extended ladder on the ground, you could ask adults to do the top five rungs and young children to do the bottom five rungs. Alternatively, use bouncy balls instead of bean bags – not at all easy if the ladder is placed on hard concrete surface! And the balls have to stay in the rungs – if they bounce out, the game is over!

95. Lucky dips

Buy lots of little, pocket toys at your local toy shop or wholesaler, preferably at a discount – make sure you tell them what you are buying the toys for as they might have old stock they can donate for free. Then put the toys in a big bucket or bin with lots of shredded newspaper inside. You could wrap the tops up beforehand as well, although this is another cost to consider as well as time-consuming. I find that as long as the toys are well covered in shredded newspaper, then it is still just as exciting for children. For a donation that is more than what the prizes cost, children put their hand into the big tubs and pull out a lucky dip toy. The good thing about not wrapping the toys up is that children can always have another go if they aren't happy with the picked toy, although this is at your discretion! Either make the game suitable for boys and girls with unisex toys for all ages in one big tub or have two separate lucky dips, one for boys and one for girls. Alternatively, divide the toys according to age (so an under fives and an under tens).

96. Splat the rat

For this fundraising game you just need a secure step-ladder, a long pipe that a rat shaped stuffed toy can slide quickly down and a baseball bat (or equivalent). It might seem like a lot of items for just one game, but once you have sourced all the materials you need, you can play this game at many future events. The person running the activity stands on the secure ladder and drops the rat shaped teddy (or a stuffed sock with sewn on eyes and tail!) down the pipe. People pay a donation to try and hit the rat before it lands on the ground! One 'splat' (i.e. hits) out of three drops wins a prize! Or you could make it harder by saying two hits out of three wins a prize!

97. Donkey / pony rides

If you live near a farm or in the countryside, why not ask a local farm, equestrian centre or horse-riding school if they could come and give pony rides at your event? Their business receives free publicity at the event and you get the money for the pony rides, or at least a percentage of the profits. Be sure you check your insurance first to make sure you are covered for any damages or accidents and that they have suitable insurance and training.

98. Bouncy castle

It doesn't cost as much as you think to hire a bouncy castle and children will gladly pay a small donation for a few minutes bouncing around with their friends. You will soon cover your costs of hiring the bouncy castle as well as raise money for your cause – but be sure you check your insurance first for accidents and damage cover.

99. Inflatable sumo wrestling

Companies that hire out bouncy castles often have other games for hire, such as inflatable sumo wrestling costumes. Why not charge people a small amount to dress up as a sumo wrestler and then wrestle each other? Not only is it very funny to watch but it is actually great fun to do – you will be surprised how many grown men enjoy this activity!

100. Welly throwing

Simple but fun! Basically, everyone throws a welly (or Wellington boot to give it their proper title!) and the person who throws it the furthest or manages to land it on a small target some distance away wins a prize! Alternatively, you could offer prizes to anyone who throws it over a certain distance. There are some people that fill the welly with custard before throwing, but that is just silly and very messy! (Remember who is going to have to clear it up afterwards!)

101. Supermarket bagging

Not so much a game, more of a fundraising activity, but consider asking your local supermarket if you and your supporters can volunteer to bag groceries or push trolleys to the cars of customers, who then donate anything they like for the service.

102. Paper airplane contest

This is a great fundraising activity for a summer's day (when there is little breeze!) but it can also be held in a sports hall. All you need are lots of sheets of coloured paper, pens to decorate the planes with and a measuring tape. Children and adults pay a small amount to make and personalise their very own paper aeroplane (which they get to keep). They then stand behind a pre-marked line and throw their paper airplane as far as possible. The airplane that flies the furthest by the end of the day wins a prize or all airplanes that pass a certain point win a smaller prize. You will find, though, that the prize isn't very important in this activity as both adults and children alike love making, decorating and then flying paper airplanes!

103. Spin a penny

For this fundraising game, you just require an old chess board, metallic marker pens and a penny. With silver and gold marker pens (as the metallic colours will show up against the black and white squares on the chess board), you write a random selection of odd and even numbers from 1 to 9, putting the higher numbers towards the edge of the board and the smaller numbers in the middle (to make it harder!). The object of the game is to spin a penny on the board and if it lands on an even number you have another go, adding up each even number it lands on until the penny lands on an odd number whereupon the game is over. If the penny spins off the board then the game is over too. The person who gets the most points at the end of the event wins a prize or anyone who scores over 30 points wins a prize.

104. Roll a dice

Very similar to the previous fundraising idea, but this time you throw a dice and keep adding the even numbers until you reach an odd. The highest score at the end of the event wins a prize, or anyone who scores more than 20 points wins a prize. Alternatively, you could run a challenge to throw sixes – who ever throws the most sixes consecutively or in a minute wins a prize.

105. Conker championship

A traditional autumn competition that involves many conkers and some strong string. Entrants buy a conker that is already attached to some string – so you will need lots of helpers collecting suitable conkers before the event! It is best to 'sell' the conkers for this activity rather than request children bring their own as

back to the organizers (sometime in the autumn) and the person whose sunflower is the tallest by this date wins a prize (maybe gardening vouchers donated by a local garden centre?). This fundraising idea also works well with vegetables such as 'the heaviest potato' or 'the longest runner bean'.

112. Gardening team

Another fundraising idea, similar to the ironing, cleaning and dog walking ideas, is to offer your gardening skills in return for a donation. If a team of volunteers gave up an hour of their time once a week for a donation towards your charity, then the amount soon builds up by the end of the year or by the end of the summer into quite a substantial sum. You could also see if a local garden centre will sponsor you, giving you a discount of plants, seeds and gardening tools.

113. Gift wrapping

Ask people for a donation in return for their presents to be gift-wrapped, with a minimum charge to cover the paper, tape, ribbons and bows. This works very well near Christmas time! Just make sure your stall is in the middle of a busy town centre so that people can have the presents they have just bought wrapped up straight away. Alternatively, ask your local shopping centre or supermarket if you could have a table in a prominent place so newly bought presents can be wrapped. Make sure you have clear signs telling everyone about the good cause you are raising money for. Also make sure you take any price tickets and labels of before wrapping!

114. Shoe shine

In the middle of a busy town or in your local supermarket or shopping centre, offer to clean people's shoes in return for a donation to your cause. If there is a team of you doing this over one day or a weekend, consider turning it into a sponsorship activity: how many pairs of shoes can be cleaned in one day? Why not ask people to sponsor you fifty pence per pair of shoes and ask your local dry cleaners, shoe repair shop or specialist cleaners if they will match the amount raised or provide all the cleaning materials free of charge in return for good publicity.

115. Heads and tails

This is a popular game that is often used as an ice-breaker at sit-down meal or dancing events. Everyone gives a donation to take part in the game, which starts with everyone standing up and putting their hands on either their bottom (for 'tails') or on their head (for 'heads'). An announcer flips a coin and if the coin lands 'heads' up, then everyone with their hands on their heads stay in the game. Everyone who guessed incorrectly and put their hands on their bottom sit down as they are now out of the game. The announcer keeps going until there is just one person left who receives a prize. The prize is usually something quite impressive such as a meal at a local restaurant or a bottle of champagne, depending on how much people paid to participate in the game at the beginning. If you had 100 people at a sit-down meal who each paid £5, even with a winning prize of £50 you will still raise £450 with no other costs and very little organization involved.

116. A grotto

A grotto can make any event very special for young children and whilst it is usually held at Christmas time and with Father Christmas, it could also be run at Easter with young children meeting the Easter Bunny to say hello and receive a little chocolate egg. Turn a small room or shed into a grotto with fairy lights and decorations that are linked to the character 'living' there – so snowflakes, holly, ivy, fake snow and a Christmas tree for Father Christmas and eggs, bunnies, chicks and spring flowers for the Easter bunny. Have a couple of helpers in fancy dress to help the children go into the grotto one at a time and then out again through a different exit, and charge parents (and their little child) a small amount to meet either Father Christmas or the Easter

Bunny to receive a small present. Magical as well as memorable, a grotto can be a great fundraiser for your cause.

117. Egg and spoon race

This is a great game for summer fairs and sport themed activity days that can either be run individually (where everyone competes against each other) or as a relay team event. Contestants pay an entry fee to compete in a running race whilst balancing an egg on a spoon. The first person over the finishing line with an unbroken egg still on their spoon wins a prize. You can make this very difficult by using a large egg such as an ostrich egg on a teaspoon and a great sponsorship idea is to have a team of people running relay laps of an athletic track balancing an egg on a spoon! See how many laps they can do in total during the course of one afternoon. It would also look fantastic if they ran in fancy dress, maybe as ducks and chickens! Imagine the publicity photos!

118. Scalextric races

Dads and sons love this game as it reminds them of the celebrity racing challenge on *Top Gear*, although mums and daughters also find it great fun! Set up a toy car racing game with a scalextric set and hold a competition to find the fastest person to do three laps around a complicated course (with everyone paying a small donation to have a go at the challenge). Times are recorded using a stop watch and written up on a display board so everyone knows the times they have to beat. The winner is revealed at the end of the event whereupon they receive their prize – preferably something car or racing related donated by the local toy shop, garage or racing school. You could even have three champions – an adult champion, an under 18s champion and an under 10 champion. Alternatively, charge people a small amount to just race against each other for three or more laps (maybe run a child versus parent competition with the parent having a car that is set to run slower than the child's car!) with the winning child getting a few sweets plus a certificate that said 'I beat my Dad at Scalextric today!'

119. Wind-up toy races

This fundraising idea is very cheap to run and is a great deal of fun. All you need is a table with a start and finish clearly marked and a wide selection of wind-up toys (once you have bought these they will come in again for future events). Basically, everyone pays a small amount to play the game and chooses one of the wind-up toys. Everyone winds up their toy at the beginning of the race and after a 'ready, steady, go' they release their wound up toy at the start line. The first toy to pass the finishing line is the winner and the person gets a small prize. This game is so much fun that children and adults play it again and again! It is also great to see and hear so many grown-ups shouting frantically to urge their toy on pass the finishing line. This game works really well if the toys do flips, go backwards or make lots of interesting moves rather than just move forward!

120. Arm wrestling competition

This fundraising idea works well at the end of a sports themed event and can be titled as 'a strongest man, woman or child competition' where contestants pit against each other through a series of knockout stages until a winner is revealed. Alternatively, one person is challenged by everyone and anyone who beats the person wins a prize. Entrants pay a minimum donation towards your charity, society, club or school for taking part and you could have a variety of winners – arm wrestling champion for male adults, female adults, under 18s and under 10s. Ask your local gym or leisure centre if they can donate some prizes to the contest, maybe a free month's membership in return for publicity at your event.

121. Tug of war

Just like the previous fundraising idea, this game works very well at the end of a sports themed event. Whilst it can be run with individuals competing against each other, similar to the previous fundraising idea, it actually works best with teams of people and makes for some excellent publicity photos (especially if each team is in fancy dress!). Contestants pay a small donation towards your charity, society, club or school to take part and through a knock-out system, the winning team or person wins a prize. This is a wonderful activity that draws in a large crowd, with spectators cheering on their favourite team and spending money at other stalls at the event. As for the prize, it doesn't have to be extrava-gant – a round of drinks from your loc al public house would be well appreciated by the adults or how about just being crowned the tug of war champions of the year?

Make and sell

Making and selling something is an excellent way of adding individuality to your fundraising as the items made in advance (or during) can be adapted to follow the theme of your event. In addition to this, homemade items add a lovely and unique personal touch to your fundraising that people would not be able to buy elsewhere.

122. Hot and cold drinks

Providing refreshments is an essential stall at any fundraising event and whilst it might seem obvious that there would be teas and coffees for sale, you would be surprised the number of fundraising events that don't capitalize on this further by offering a wider variety of hot and cold drinks for adults and children. It doesn't cost much more to run, but by offering hot chocolate, herbal teas and decaffeinated coffee you are ensuring that there is something for everyone on offer, no matter what their tastes are. However, it doesn't have to be just hot drinks on offer. Remember to offer diluted squash for children and why not consider running a healthy juice stall during a summer event or how about homemade lemonade? Not only is it different and makes your refreshments stall that little bit more interesting to the people attending, freshly made juice and ice-cold homemade lemonade are refreshingly bliss on a summer's day!

123. Food

As well as drinks, always ensure you provide plenty of opportunity for people attending your event to purchase food. This could be a 'made to order' sandwich and salad stall, an American style hot dog and beefburger stand, or even a hog roast on a turning spit. Remember to cater for vegetarians and vegans and try and link it to the theme of your event, so curries and naan bread during an Indian themed event held on Gandhi's birthday (2nd October). Think healthily about the food options you prefer as well as the people attending (children might not want spicy lentils for example!) and also remember desserts with an ice-cream, stand perhaps! If the cost of food, preparing the food and volunteers to serve it up is proving difficult then ask a local restaurant or catering company to come in and provide the food with a percentage of the profits being donated to your charity, school, society or club.

124. Sweet stall

Homemade sweets are a real treat at a fundraising event that very few people can resist! Ask your supporters to bring in their sweet delights for a traditional homemade confectionary stall of fudge, truffles, treacle toffee and toffee apples. You could even dig out an old recipe book from decades ago and try some forgotten childhood favourites such as peppermint creams, cherry and coconut squares and Everton toffees!

125. Cake stall

No event is complete without a homemade cake stall full of sponge cakes, fairy cakes, gingerbread, fruit cakes, lemon drizzle cakes, scones, biscuits, chocolate brownies and so much more! Ask members of your congregation, school, society or friends and family to donate their baking to a cake and biscuit stall, which you can dress in a colourful gingham table cloth and matching serviettes to make it look inviting. Alternatively, ask a local farm or cake shop to put on a stall of their goodies with a split of the profits going to your good cause. Just make sure that any cakes or biscuits containing nuts or gluten are clearly marked due to allergies.

126. Star cakes

This is more of an activity but as it involved making something and then selling them (even though there is a game attached!), I thought I would add it here! Ask friends, family, parishioners and parents to make as many fairy cakes as possible. Before the event begins, on half of the cakes draw a star on the bottom of their paper case with a marker or gold pen (stickers don't stick I am afraid!). Charge a small donation per cake and if the person chooses one with a star underneath they receive a few sweets as well as the lovely cake to eat! Even if people don't win the sweets, they still get to enjoy the cake! Handy hint: make sure you have enough sweets for the number of stars drawn (with quite a few spare as I find you often need extra sweets for some reason!)

127. Decorate biscuits

Just like the previous fundraising idea, ask friends, family, parents and supporters to make as many plain biscuits as possible. At the event ask for a small donation for people (usually children!) to decorate a plain biscuit in lots of lovely icing and sprinkles. They then get to eat the biscuit they have created or give it to someone else to enjoy! Fun to make and fun to eat, this is quite a simple (although somewhat messy) activity that raises valuable funds for your charity, society, club or school.

128. Popcorn

The smell of warm, fresh popcorn will be a sure hit with people attending your event and is certainly something different to offer them. You can hire specialist popcorn machinery for your event, or you can get a pan, some hot oil and some popping corn to save money. And remember to provide something to serve the popcorn in such as paper cones.

129. Bread stall

For something a little bit different, why not put on a homemade bread stall? Ask your supporters to bring in a homemade loaf each and just see how many varieties come in: rolls, bloomers, olive and sundried tomato bread, ciabattas, rosemary bread, bagels, wholemeal or white, naan, baguettes and even fruit bread.

You can then either sell the loaves and rolls to people attending your event or put on a 'make your own' sandwich stall. Any bread left over could be donated to your local homeless charity for giving away. Not only is the smell of bread wonderful, this fundraising stall is great at harvest time. If baking bread isn't possible then ask a local baker for their support with a share of the profits made during the event being donated to your good cause.

130. Jams and chutneys

Who can resist buying a jar of homemade strawberry jam, lemon curd, orange and lemon marmalade or apple and date chutney at a charity or school fair? And the good thing about jams, chutneys and preserves is that they don't perish quickly so any leftover jars can be sold at your next event too. Also, pop it by a cheese stall from your local farm shop and you have a winning combination!

131. Reindeer food

This is a great one for a Christmas Fair. Mix oats with glitter and spoon it into small organza or paper bags. Then tie it up tight (so the mixture doesn't escape!) and attach a label saying 'Reindeer Food', or the following rhyme: *"Sprinkle on your lawn at night, the moon will make it sparkle bright! As Santa's reindeer fly and roam, this will guide them to your home!"* You could even do something similar for the Easter Bunny!

132. Greeting cards

Christmas cards, Happy Easter cards, New Year cards, Mother's Day and Father's Day cards, Valentine cards, new school cards, birthday cards or just plain inside but beautifully decorated cards can be made cheaply with a local printer or one of the numerous companies online to be sold at any of your events. Cards drawn by children in your society, charity, club, congregation or school are particularly popular with their friends and relatives and companies that specialise in this will give your school or charity a percentage of all orders taken.

133. Postcards

Cheaper than cards but just as effective, why not design and sell your own postcards to raise money for your cause? You could even ask local shops, post offices and newsagents to purchase a batch of the postcards to sell in their stores. Just like greeting cards, make sure your good cause and what you are raising money for is clearly mentioned and pictures drawn by children associated with your charity, hospice, society or school work particularly well.

134. Calendars

Another item that can be made and then sold at events is a calendar. This works very well at the end of a year, from autumn onwards, and should be sold at a higher price than the cost to make so that a good profit is raised for your fundraising fund. There are numerous companies and printers who will offer a school, charity, society or club a good printing deal to help keep costs down and each page could be designed by a different child or adult at your charity, society or school to highlight the different aspects of the work you do. You should also consider allocating some space on the calendar for advertising, maybe in the top corner or along the bottom. If you sold advertising space to a local company on each page per month, you might be able to cover the total cost of printing the calendar, ensuring all income received from sales is pure profit. Maybe you could create the next hugely successful Women Institute's calendar that inspired the film *Calendar Girls*?

135. Cookbook

Another popular fundraising idea is to create your own recipe book. Ask your supporters for their favourite original recipes and then publish them in a cookbook that can be sold either at events using a local printer or online with the use of a self-publishing company such as Lulu. Just like making and selling calendars, ensure the cost of producing the cookbook is less than the retail price of the book and, if sold locally, why not include advertisements in the book to help cover the printing costs? You could also create specialist recipe books for specific stalls or themes, so a traditional sweet and confectionary recipe book that can also be sold of a 'Sweets of yesterday' stall. So people can sample the delights and then buy the recipe!

136. Books

Following on from the previous entry, why not publish an annual school achievement book with a piece of writing from every pupil in the school? Or a collection of poems on a theme connected to your charity's work? There are a number of publishers who publish books to raise money for charities, including the publisher of this book, Nell James Publishers. Alternatively, consider publishing it with a no-cost self-publishing company such as Lulu or with an independent printer (to sell locally or direct to your supporters).

137. Advertising booklet / directory

If you have a wide mailing list connected to your society, charity or school, then you might want to consider creating an advertising booklet, which is distributed free to your supporters but companies pay a small charge to be included. You could even create your own local directory (maybe a specialist one of trades people or mobile beauticians, manicurists and hairdressers?) and distribute it free to households in your neighbourhood, with companies paying a small amount to be listed.

138. Tea towels

Whilst tea towels are often considered a fundraiser of the past, you will be surprised how well a lovely designed tea towel can sell – after all, everyone uses them and if you follow a modern pattern or design it with a retro 1950s feel, it will certainly be a hit with the public. Why not ask the children in your school or society to design a section of the tea towel or use their hand prints to cover the fabric of the tea towel? Companies that specialise in manufacturing tea towels will often give a discount for good fundraising causes and if you ensure the tea towel is not specific to one event, then they can be sold again and again at future events.

139. Scented bags for drawers

Like the previous entry on tea towels, scented bags for underwear cupboards and linen closest are not considered as popular as they use to be. Yet they will always appeal to a certain sector of the public, especially if they have been created by children your charity or hospice have helped. Just sew some dried lavender into a little silk or organza purse and whoever buys the scented bags will be reminded of your good cause every time they smell the lovely natural fragrance.

140. Knitting

If anyone connected to your fundraising is good at knitting, then why not have a knitting stall, full of scarves, hats, cosy cardigans and baby bonnets for people to buy? You could even run this as a sponsorship activity – how many scarves can be knitted in one weekend – and then all the scarves are sold at an event, raising money twice for your good cause.

141. Stone paper weights

If you live near the coast, then why not collect some smooth pebbles from the beach to paint and varnish and sell as paper weights? Not only do the stones become useful and pretty paper weights for someone's office or desk, but they will continue to remind people of your fundraising aims and raise money at very little cost. You could even run this as an activity with children and adults decorating the stones at your event for a minimum

making activity, similar to the flower pot fundraising idea. Why not ask a local company to sponsor the reverse side of the coasters in order to cover the manufacturing costs? Or if your fundraising is associated with children, why not use the children's handprints to personalize the coasters, or a pet's paws if raising money for an animal charity?

148. DVD

If you are putting on a performance, show, play, pantomime or nativity, why not ask someone to record it professionally and sell it to supporters, parents and the public as a DVD? Ensure you have everyone's permission first before recording. Alternatively, make a DVD of your charity, club, society or school's achievements, goals, success stories for the year and sell this for a small donation to supporters.

149. CD

Just like the previous fundraising idea, why not record a CD of your church, school, society or club choir to sell to supporters? You will need everyone's permission before recording commences, with a parent or guardian's consent for any under 18s. Who knows, the next St Winifred's choir, Charlotte Church or Aled Jones could be found amongst your choir members!

150. Programmes

If you are running an event where people are putting on a performance (whether it is a theatre production, nativity, dance show, talent show or musical night), a great fundraising opportunity exists in the sale of programmes. Detailing the schedule of the evening, cast members, brief biographies, any background story as well as the reason for your fundraising, a programme will certainly be bought by the majority of people attending the performance. The programme could also contain advertising from local businesses and if their contribution covered the printing costs at least then all the money made from the sale of the programmes would mean pure profit for your good cause. In addition to advertising, ensure you promote any future fundraising events you are holding in the programme.

151. Stop signs

A 'Stop here Santa' sign is a sure winner at a Christmas Fair and can be either signs that go outside (for example, a wooden pole with a painted wooden cut-out of Santa nailed on) or hung on a bedroom door like a door hanger. The signs should be made well in advance and sold either with a pre-order form or at an actual event. Why not also consider a 'Stop Easter Bunny' sign too?

152. Soap making

Making homemade, natural soap is a great way of raising money as it smells divine and in an age where everyone is trying to reduce the amount of chemicals their skin absorb, it is a real crowd pleaser.

153. Bracelets

A collection of beads and some wool is all you need to make some simple bracelets for your fundraising event. You could even run it as a 'make and sell' activity with children (and adults) making their very own bracelet. If your event has a colour theme then the beads and wool could reflect these colours. You could also tie it to a Valentine event with little heart beads or a Mother's Day event with 'I love you Mum' bracelets.

154. Personalised hair bands

Just like previous entries, you can buy plain hair bands from a wholesaler at a discount or ask a local hairdresser or accessory shop to supply the hair bands at cost price in return for publicity for their business. You can then run an activity for children and adults to personalise the hair bands with felt, stickers, sequins, glitter and ribbon for a small charge. Not only is it fun to make but everyone gets to take home with them something pretty and memorable from your event. Make sure you do some hair bands in advance so you have lots of colourful, interesting and pretty hair bands decorating your stall (which you can also sell in case people don't want to make their own).

155. Personalised T-shirts

By purchasing special transfer paper and plain t-shirts, you can run a 'make your own t-shirt' activity. Children and adults choose their design from a wide selection or design their own on a computer that is then printed out on the transfer paper. The design is then ironed on to the t-shirt, creating something that is unique to the person as well as your event.

156. Personalised bags

Just like above, but instead of ironing designs onto t-shirts, why not iron designs on to plain cotton bags, which can be bought in bulk and at a discount from wholesalers? You could do the bags in advance with designs that include the promotional tag line of your charity, society or school or you could create a wide general selection which would appeal to a wider market. If you have the facilities during your event, why not run this as a 'make and sell' activity, with people creating their own designs and personalising the bags further with sequins, ribbons, pens and felt pens?

157. Badges

Collect wild lavender or another scented flower, tie it together with some ribbon, attach a safety pin to the back and there you have a gorgeous, scented flower badge to sell at your event. If wild flowers are tricky or expensive to acquire, just use some strong card already cut into a variety of shapes that can be personalised, decorated, coloured, laminated and attached to a safety pin. This fundraising 'make and sell' idea is a winner for children at all events throughout the year.

Buy and sell

Sometimes it isn't always possible to make things in advance or during your event or even to ask for donations. Sometimes you need to buy items at a discounted price and sell them on for a profit. There are many items you can purchase that can be connected to your charity, society, club or school, either branded with your logo or linked to the theme of your event. Following are just some suggestions of buying in bulk and selling on to the public and your supporters for a profit.

158. Branded merchandise

Anything can be branded with your logo and aim (mugs, pens, t-shirts, coasters, tea towels, bags) and can be sold at a marked up price at your event for a profit. Ensure that no dates are included and that any branding isn't specific to one event, so if the items don't sell at that particular Summer Fair or at your autumn fundraising event, they can always be sold at Christmas or in the New Year.

159. Rubber wrist bands

This is a popular and contemporary fundraising item that can be bought in bulk in a variety of colours (or one colour connected to your charity, society, club or school) with your charity's name or logo printed on. They can be sold as an accessory for people to wear and show their support or can even be sold as part of an entry ticket to your charity, school or village event, with the cost of the rubber wrist band included in the entry price.

160. Plant sale

Buy plants at a wholesaler or at cost from your local garden centre and sell them for a marked up price at your spring fair. You could ask your local plant nursery if they could create an order form that you can distribute to parents, parishioners and supporters. Once the orders and money has been taken, your charity, society or school receives a percentage of the profits made. You could do this throughout the year: spring bulbs, summer flowers, autumn colours and even Christmas trees. Alternatively, ask a local garden centre to set up a stall at your event with a percentage of takings donated to your charity.

161. A rose for 'Rosie'

If you are raising money for a children's charity or hospice, then why not personalise it by using one of the children's name (if it is the same as a name of a flower) and associating it with a gift? You could buy cut roses from a flower wholesaler or florist, wrap it in some lovely cellophane and ribbon and then sell it at a marked up price – 'A rose for Rosie'! You could also use this for lilies, daisies and poppies. This works wonderfully at spring and summer events as well as for Mother's Day. It also creates a lovely personal touch to your fundraising that the local press will probably like to cover in a feature.

162. Toys

If you contact a local manufacturing company of toys and explain what you are doing (i.e. raising money for your charity, school, club or society) they are likely to sell you a bulk quantity of toys at a substantial discount in return for publicity about their toys. You can then sell the toys for a marked up price (but still less than the recommended retail price, so passing on some of the discount to your supporters) at your fundraising event or direct through an order form. You could also consider contacting your local toy shop to see if they can do something similar. The good thing about toys is that they don't go out of date and there are always new children joining your club, society, school or church and attending your fundraising events for the first time. If you are raising money for a children's hospice, you could try and purchase a toy that had a personal or significant meaning for the children you are supporting, such as a sensory toy like a kaleidoscope or a musical toy. If you are raising money for your school, then you can choose an educational toy or something that is linked to the curriculum.

163. Books

Just like the previous fundraising idea about buying toys and selling them on for a profit, you can do the same thing with books. In fact, it is actually easier to do this with books. You can purchase box sets of books from discount book companies such as The Book People (www.thebookpeople.co.uk) and then sell the books individually at a higher price to make a profit. Make sure you pass on some of the discount to your supporters, parents and the public as then they will be pleased and will purchase books from you again in the future. You could also contact publishers regarding any stock they are planning to 'remainder', which is when it will be pulped. They often sell this stock at rock bottom prices or will give it away for free, so ask to be added to their mailing list regarding any remaindered or discounted stock. It is also great publicity for the publisher as they are then linked with a charitable or fundraising cause. And it doesn't have to just be children publishers – contact local history publishers and fiction presses to see what is available.

164. Balloons

A very simple item you can buy and then sell at your event is balloons. Either shiny, big helium ones or just standard air ones, attached to some string. It is very cheap to run and if you don't price them too expensive, they will sell well to children and parents. If you don't have enough volunteers to sell balloons at your event, then tie them to the gazebos or table legs of your stalls. Not only will it brighten up the whole event but it also means the person selling cakes or running a lucky dip stall can also sell a few balloons. You could even get balloons printed with your charity, school, club or society name and logo on. Just like other items, don't mention one event or date on the balloon to ensure any unsold balloons can be used again at future events.

165. Tuck shop / penny sweets

A sweet shop is a great way of people using up their spare change and keeps children quiet for a minute or two. You can sell crisps and cans of pop, bought in bulk from a local wholesaler, and if you buy tubs of sweets and paper bags, you can make up little bags of sweets in advance to the value of 20p and 50p. As sweets have a long shelf life, any sweets not sold at your first event can be sold again at your next one.

Themes and events

The following chapter gives examples of all the different events and themes you can run throughout the year. Remember that at each event organised you could sell a programme (which includes local advertising inside), sell drinks and food, play games, ask for donations, have a raffle and so much more. Here is a list of seasonal events (arranged by date from 1st January to 31st December) and suggestions for various activities you could run:

166. Burns Supper
(25th January)
Enjoy the poetry of the great Scottish Robert Burns with some haggis, whiskey and a recital of Burns' unforgettable poetry. You could wear a kilt for the day in the office, run a 'design your own tartan' competition or have an evening of Scottish music and dancing.

167. Australia Day
(26th January)
On a cold, wet and possibly snowy winter's day in January, wear beach shorts in the office and hold a barbeque outside. Or have a sponsored boomerang contest, learn the didgeridoo or have an orienteering contest to find the kangaroo. For schools, why not do a sponsored 'Facts about Australia' contest and maybe contact a school in Australia who children can write too?

168. Chinese New Year
(Late January – mid-February)
Sell Chinese food, put on a performance from Chinese folklore with dancing dragons, sell fortune cookies and beautiful lanterns, make and sell bookmarks with Chinese writing on and even have a sponsored great wall of China walk on a treadmill.

169. Japan's National Day
(11th February)
Sell sushi and sashimi, wear a kimono all day, have a sponsored sumo costume race or contest in inflatable sumo suits, run a sponsored Japanese endurance challenge, have a sponsored Mount Fuji climb on a treadmill, or even hold your own Japanese tea ceremony followed by some karaoke! You could even make and sell origami paper cranes, personalised Japanese bookmarks or door signs or even Japanese face painting.

170. Valentine's Day
(14th February)
Sell roses, origami paper hearts, fairy cakes decorated with hearts on top or hold a Valentine's disco, find the Queen of Hearts game (see page 34) or how about a speed dating night? Why not consider organising a sponsored 'hug-a-thon' or the largest group hug?

171. Presidents day or Washington's birthday
(The third Monday of February)
Have a sponsored Presidents of the USA quiz, make and sell American food, make American flag tea towels or coasters for people to buy and even have a American line dancing and music evening!

172. Shrove Tuesday / Pancake Day
(46 days before Easter)
It has to be everything to do with pancakes on this day! Pancakes (or crepes) to make, sell and eat with lots of different fillings: sweet fillings such as lemon and sugar, jam or chocolate, or savoury ones such as cheese, ham and mushrooms. Why not have a pancake and frying pan race followed by a sponsored pancake toss?

173. St David's Day
(1st March)

Celebrate Wales with lamb and leek cuisine, sell bunches of daffodils, learn some Welsh place names for a geography test, or sponsor people to climb Snowdonia. If you can't get to North Wales to climb Snowdonia, then why not have a sponsored climb on a step machine?

174. St Patrick's Day
(17th March)

Everybody loves St Patrick's Day: a great day to enjoy all things Irish – Guinness, whiskey, Irish music, Irish dancing! Why not put on your own *Riverdance* show, wear nothing but green for the day or even write your own limericks for an Irish literary night?

175. Mothers Day
(Three weeks before Easter Sunday, usually in March)

Fundraise by having an event that celebrates motherhood. Put on a play, sell flowers, have a pampering evening with an external company (you receive a share of the profits from any beauty items sold at the event – see page 91 for a list of companies), or even get the children to do a sponsored 'washing-up and tidy bedrooms' for a week! You could also create personalised stone paper weights, bookmarks, origami hearts or bracelets for people to buy for their Mum.

176. Easter Fair
(A moveable date but usually between March and April)

A popular one for children with a hunt the Easter Egg game, an Easter egg tombola, a visit from the Easter Bunny, egg decorating, an egg roll down a hill race and you mustn't forget the egg and spoon race! You could also put on a play about the Easter story (selling programmes, food and refreshments plus a raffle during the interval) or how about a sponsored 'quit it' for the whole of Lent - maybe coffee, sweets or chocolate. You might even encourage someone to stop smoking!

177. St George's Day
(23rd April)
As this is England's national day, why not have a medieval England theme and a 'galloping knight race' (i.e. on a pogo stick or using a decorated mop or broom)? Dress up in medieval costume for the day, sell red and white cakes, find the Knight in a pack of cards game (like the Queen of Hearts game on page 34), and maybe have an old English poetry recital with some Morris dancing?

178. South Africa's National Day
(27th April)
Celebrating South Africa's first democratic general election in 1994, why not use this event to highlight charities in Africa and human rights? Have a sponsored silence or fast, climb up Table Mountain (on a treadmill) and sell South African food such as biltong, boerewors and redbush tea. You could also run a 'facts about South Africa' test.

179. May Day
(1st May)
The first of May is a great time to have a village fete or a community gathering, selling cakes and drinks alongside lots of lovely outdoor activities for everyone to either watch or participate in. You could dance round a Maypole, put on a play and maybe have a 'balloon release' race (page 32).

180. Queen of England's birthday
(1st or 2nd Saturday in June)
Just like the previous entry, have a truly British fundraising event on the Queen's birthday, selling teas, sandwiches and scones

followed by a sponsored quiz on the Kings and Queens of England and the United Kingdom.

181. Father's Day
(The third Sunday of June)
Celebrate fatherhood by organising a sport outing to a football, rugby, cricket, motor racing or horse racing event (the coach and entry fee included in a ticket price, which also raises a small profit for your charity). Alternatively, organise your own event of sporting activities, selling food and drinks and running lots of sporting challenges finishing with an arm-wrestling contest!

182. Canada Day
(1st July)
A great Canadian event that could be decorated in red and white maple leaf flags and balloons. Sell waffles and maple syrup, have a sponsored hike as a Rocky Mountain ranger or a sponsored lake swim or how about a grizzly bear tea party?

183. France Day
(14th July)
A wonderful continental day that could include a sponsored speak French for 24 hours, a sponsored bike ride like the Tour d'France, sell croissants and French food, perform a play about a particular period in French history or dress all day as a stereotypical or famous French person!

184. Sport's Day
(July)
Whether your fundraising is connected to a school or not, a sports day for children or a 'retro sports day' for adults is great fun! Run traditional school races such as the egg and spoon race, the sack race and the three-legged race. Sell drinks and food as well as put on a variety of stalls to keep spectators entertained,

including a raffle and some bean bag sport activities (see page 42 for ideas).

185. Summer fairs
(Anytime in July/August)
Celebrate the summer with a glorious fair. Bunting, bouncy castles, funny races, face painting, homemade lemonade, pony rides and lovely food to eat such as strawberries and ice-cream. For adults, why not put on a 'play in the park', a sponsored walk or cycle (that ends at the fair) or a 5km run around the parameters of the fair?

186. India's Independence Day
(15th August)
A great excuse to make and sell some wonderful curries, naan bread and poppadoms! Have some traditional Indian dancing for entertainment, wear a sari all day, have an 'Indian' quiz night (whilst serving the curry!) and maybe arrange a performance or a play about an Indian religious story.

187. Harvest festival
(Can be anytime in autumn)
Similar to the USA's Thanksgiving, this is a celebration to give thanks for the reaping and gathering of grain. Celebrate it by selling handmade corn dolls (made from a harvested sheaf of corn) with people donating food that can be distributed to the needy. Some people even hold a scarecrow festival, with a competition to find the best scarecrow!

188. Spain's National Day
(12th October)
Serve up paella and tapas, have a Spanish music and flamenco night, make Spanish fans to sell and have a sponsored 'bull-fight' with someone pretending to be the bull!

189. Halloween

(31st October)
A spooky yet fun event! Hold a 'Halloween disco' for children or adults, wear fancy dress for the day, sell pumpkin pie, pumpkin soup and ghost shaped biscuits.

190. Bonfire night / Guy Fawkes night

(5th November)
I love this event! It is one of my favourites! The smell of toffee apples, treacle toffee and parkin; the sounds and lights of a firework display and bonfire. Why not put on a Guy Fawkes play or organise a history quiz about it? And don't forget 'A Penny for the Guy'!

191. Thanksgiving

(The fourth Thursday in November)
Offer a feast of food to paying guests in order to give thanks and put on a play about the Pilgrim Fathers. You could even hold a States of America or a Presidents of America quiz.

192. St Andrew's Day

(30th November)
Scotland's national day, so why not serve haggis, have a whiskey tasting session, wear a kilt for the day, toss the caber and hold a céilidh?

193. Christmas fairs

(Anytime in December before Christmas Eve)
A perfect and magical event for fundraising: Santa's grotto, a secret Santa room (see page 25), sell reindeer food (see page 56), serve mince pies and mulled wine for a donation and have a choir carol singing in the background to create an atmosphere. Plus the usual stalls selling Christmas presents, children lucky dips, a raffle, a chocolate or bottle tombola, decorate star biscuits, name the teddy (preferably a fluffy snowman or reindeer!), make 'Stop

here Santa' door handles, put on a nativity play, sell bunches of mistletoe and holly wreaths, ask a garden centre to sell Christmas trees for a percentage of sales and even guess the weight of a homemade Christmas cake! So many ideas!

194. Pantomime
(December/January)
Why not put on your own pantomime? Sell tickets, drinks, food and even have a raffle during the interval or at the end.

Following are fundraising themes and events that can be held at any time of the year:

195. Plays
Why not put on a play? Not only do you get money from your ticket sales, but also for any refreshments and programmes (including advertising) sold during the interval. You can also hold a raffle on the night of the performance (drawn in the interval or at the end).

196. Talent show
Alternatively, hold a local talent contest with singers, magicians, comedians and bands. Advertise for a variety of acts (with a cash prize as an incentive), charge an entry fee for spectators or ask for donations and you can have a great deal of fun as well as raise money from the sale of refreshments and programmes.

197. Concert
Put on a concert. You never know what hidden talents your colleagues and friends might have! If you are part of a choir, then put on a performance, wonderful at any time of the ear but especially lovely at Christmas time. Tickets could be sold in advance or on the door as well as the usual programmes, re-freshments and other games.

198. Music night

Alternatively, pay someone to put on a concert or a music night. Tribute bands can be great fun as well as draw in a big crowd, from whom you can collect donations, sell refreshments and have other activities and games on at the same time. You could also organise a decade night (such as the 1970s, 1980s, a rock n roll night or the swinging sixties). Choose a decade, pick music to suit and then encourage people to come in fancy dress. Tickets can be sold in advance or on the door, as well as food and drinks during the evening plus a few extra games (raffle, the best fancy dress costume etc.). For a more relaxed music night, why not have a night dedicated to one particular genre (opera, jazz, blues or musicals) with a band and food?

199. Battle of the bands

Why not run your own mini-Glastonbury with a competition between local bands to see who the best is (voted for by the audience)? Money can be raised from entry tickets, the sale of food and refreshments as well as a variety of stalls surrounding the stage.

200. Award ceremonies

A school or society (such as a dance club, gymnastics club or swimming club) could hold an award ceremony every year, with the sale of refreshments and programmes raising money to support your fundraising activities. At the award ceremony, you could give the winners certificates and medals as well as put on a swimming demonstration, ballet performance or school recital to all the proud parents.

201. Street party

Don't wait for the next royal coronation or wedding and have your own street party to support your local hospice, school or charity. With colourful bunting decorating the neighbourhood, a wide variety of stalls, games and refreshments, not only will you create a great community atmosphere but you will also raise valuable funds for your local charity or organisation.

202. Local festivals / community fairs

If the above is too hard to organise, then why not have a stall or two at a local fair or festival? Homemade cakes and refreshment stalls do particularly well, but why not consider an awareness stall about your charity and sell branded merchandise? Alternatively, offer fun games for people to try for a donation and promote the work that is done by your charity or society.

203. Dinner dance

These are a very popular ticketed event that can raise a lot of money – however, they do require quite a lot of organising and promotion to ensure you get enough people attending. Whilst having the dinner or the dance, why not run some other activities, such as a raffle or the 'heads and tails' game (page 49)?

204. Dancing / disco

A night of dancing is very popular and tickets can be sold in advance with refreshments, games and other activities available during the evening. Why not try different types of dancing – a Scottish céilidh, Irish dancing, American line dancing, salsa, ballroom? Discos are thoroughly enjoyed by children and can be tagged to other events (such as a Valentine's Disco, a Halloween Bop, a Christmas Shindig). Sell tickets in advance or on the door as well as the usual refreshments and sweets on the night. You could even run party games and a raffle.

205. Masked ball

For an evening of the upmost glamour, why not organise your very own masked ball? With a fancy dress theme such as Kings and Queens, you could hold your very own Venetian ball with prizes for the best costume, the 'heads and tails' game (page 49) and a raffle.

206. Karaoke competition

If singing is more popular than dancing, then why not run your own karaoke night (on a Japanese themed evening?) or an 'X-Factor' competition with refreshments, games and food on sale? You never know, there could be a star amongst your pupils, society members or charity supporters!

If physical activities are more popular with your supporters than music, dancing and singing, then why not organise a sport themed event, where individuals or teams pay an entry fee to participate and a cash prize is offered to the winners? It is all about having an attraction that people will come and either watch or participate in, thus raising money and awareness about your charity. Once you have created 'a draw' and you have a crowd of people at your event, you can then raise more funds through a variety of spectator activities (games, food, drinks, raffle, donation buckets, face-painting etc.).

207. Charity golf day

With the support of a local golf club and the lure of a cash prize plus a possible trophy, you will attract a large golfing crowd who you can then tempt with a range of additional fundraising stalls.

208. Bowls tournament

Either ten pin bowling, skittles, or grass bowls – which ever you choose, you can create a strong contest by having either individuals or teams play as part of a knock-out competition.

209. Football tournament (5 a side)

Create a knock out tournament that can be held over one day – for example, 20 minute games. You can sell personalised t-shirts to the teams, refreshments to the spectators as well as put on a variety of activity and fun stalls to keep everyone entertained. Let's just hope it doesn't go to penalties!

210. Darts tournament

A darts knock-out competition that can either be played as individuals or teams, with food and games put on for spectators and participators.

211. Wimbledon

A charity tennis knock-out tournament can be very competitive, whether it is mixed, men, ladies, juniors singles or doubles matches being played. Keep the matches short by just playing one set. Why not also consider a table tennis or badminton tournament? You could also sell iced tea, homemade lemonade and strawberries and cream to the spectators.

212. Cricket charity contest

As above, but keep games short by limiting the number of bowls thrown. This way more teams can play and all the games are played on the same day. You could even have a local knockout contest via local villages and raise money from the sale of refreshments, a raffle and activities for the spectators.

If sport doesn't appeal to your supporters, consider a more cultural event by organising one of the following activities. Money can be raised by an entry fee plus the sale of refreshments:

213. Gallery or art show

If you have a suitable venue, ask a local art group or artist if they would like to put on a show of their work. You could then sell their artwork and retain a small commission on everything sold at the event for your charity, society, church or school.

214. Public talks / demonstrations

Every village and town has a plethora of speakers, whether they are local historians, experts in a certain field, travellers, writers or artists. Ask them to support your charity by giving a free talk or demonstration. Tickets could be sold in advance and refreshments sold during the event.

215. Local historical walk

Ask a local history expert to give a guided walk around your town, city or village. The walk and talk could be free but refreshments could be sold at the beginning, middle or end of the walk.

216. Wine tasting evening

This is very popular. Your local wine merchant is likely to offer the wine at a discount as well as recommend a suitable expert. You can make a profit from any wine sold on the night or sell tickets to hear the expert talk about wines from a particular region or how to match wines with certain foods.

217. Book club

Set up your own book club. Whilst membership to the club will be free, the sale of twenty coffee, teas and snacks every fortnight over a period of time can add quite a bit to the fundraising account. You could even get local authors to come and give a talk at your club.

There are endless other possibilities to draw in a crowd and any of the following ideas can be combined with other events previously mentioned in this chapter or held on their own:

218. Jumble sales & car boots

Either charge people an amount per stall at an advertised jumble sale or ask for donations from visitors attending. The sale of refreshments to stall owners as well as customers should also be tapped. Either rent out your car park for a car boot (charging a fee per car and selling refreshments) or invite supporters to bring their cars and donate a percentage of their profits from the event to your charity or cause.

219. Auction

Ask local companies, shops, business and supporters to donate items for an auction in return for publicity. Make sure you advertise the auction thoroughly in advance in order to draw in a crowd, promoting the top items being auctioned so that interested people will attend on the day.

220. Auction of promises

If donations are not forthcoming, donate a particular skill you have or some of your valuable time. An hour's ironing? An afternoon of gardening? A home-cooked meal? A taxi trip into town on a Saturday night? All of these can attract quite a price!

221. Singles dating night

Why not hold a speed dating night or a singles evening? Make it a ticketed event or pay on the door and sell drinks and snacks for the singletons. You could even organise a disco or a meal during the evening. Just think, your fundraising could be the start of some lovely romances!

222. Magic / Entertainment show

Ask a magician, entertainer or children's entertainer to put on a show for either adults or children for a reduced fee. You could sell tickets, refreshments and promote the work you and your charity, society, club or school are doing. The entertainer would also get considerable publicity as well as their name associated with a good cause.

223. Coffee morning

A simple tea, coffee and cake morning can raise solid funds as well as provide a regular social event for people. People can either pay for any drinks or cakes they purchase, or pay a donation on entry which includes a hot drink and sweet treat.

224. Quiz night - question of sport, university challenge

All you need is a list of general knowledge questions (or themed questions linked to the date the quiz is held on or the causes you are supporting) and a cash prize. Teams pay an entry fee to participate and refreshments (both food and drinks) are sold on the night too. You could even sell raffle tickets for a draw that can be taken at the interval. The quiz could be held on a themed night, such as the anniversary of Gandhi's birthday (2nd October), and curries could be served at the interval or while the answers are being marked. Quizzes are very popular and if you promote it well in your local community and amongst your supporters you can get a good turnout.

225. Bingo

Bingo nights are great fun and appeal to children as well as to adults! Cards and balls can be bought online and once you have got them in, they can be used again and again and again and again...! Participators pay an amount per game and prizes are awarded to the first person to shout 'bingo', when all the numbers on their card have been called! The prizes are usually cash prizes but if this is too expensive then consider offering vouchers donated by local businesses in exchange for publicity.

226. Nature walk

A nature walk (with a local walking guide and refreshments on sale) is a lovely event in all seasons. In fact, the same walk can be done in all four seasons as the difference in nature, wildlife and foliage can be quite distinct. Why not collect leaves or stones along the way and then provide tables for children to decorate them at the end of the walk, or draw around them on pieces of paper, to create a nature file? They could then research the names of the trees the leaves have fallen from. You could also provide paper and crayons for the children (and adults) to do some leaf rubbings to take away with them as a record of an enjoyable day out.

227. English garden party

With cucumber sandwiches, scones and tea, homemade lemonade and fresh strawberries with cream, this is a delightful summer event where a croquet competition could be played, a puppet show put on for the children and maybe even an English Romantic poet recital.

228. Craft show

Either a craft show of items already made specifically in advance of the event for purchasing or a craft show that teaches people the basics of basket weaving, embroidery, knitting, watercolours, soap making, candle carving, card marking, origami, flower arranging etc. You could also run a variety of 'make and sell' activities as listed on pages 53-64, notably book marks, door hangers and personalised bags.

229. Teddy bear's picnic

One for the little ones! For a small fee, invite toddler groups to come for a lovely picnic in your local park with picnic blankets to sit on, little triangle jam sandwiches and juice to enjoy and lots of fun games to play. It is a great way for new parents to come and meet other parents, for friendships to be formed as well as raise money (and awareness) for your worthwhile cause. Remind everyone to bring along a teddy too!

230. Mr. & Mrs. Evening

Compile a list of questions and (along with a sound-proof booth or a separate room) hold a very memorable Mr. & Mrs. evening. After a series of questions and knock-out rounds the winning couple who knows each other the best wins a prize (preferably a romantic meal donated by a local restaurant). Money can be raised at this event from food and drink sales, the 'heads and tails' game (page 49) and a raffle, along with any donations made or a small minimum donation to take part.

231. Fashion show

Ask your local clothes store to put on a fashion show with the clothes being shown available to buy during the evening for a discount of the recommended retail price (with a share of the takings donated to your cause). You could also sell refreshments, food and hold a raffle during the event. Alternatively, ask the fashion students at your local college, high school or university to present their work to a paying audience?

232. Eurovision party

Celebrate the Eurovision Song Contest by having a sweepstake on the winning country as well as those who receive 'null points'! You could even have a disco (to Eurovision music) with a raffle and drinks on sale. Why not encourage participators to come in fancy dress based on the different countries singing with the best costume winning a prize?

233. Your very own 'Crufts' / pet show

Organise your own 'Crufts' but for all pets not just dogs. Every-one pays an entry fee which goes towards a cash prize for the winners, with more money raised from side-line activities and the sale of refreshments. You could also ask your local pet store to sponsor the event by either providing vouchers or prizes in return for publicity or by being the judge during the event. This is a great fundraising idea if you are raising money for animal welfare causes.

234. Organise outings / Day trips

Why not organise outings with a local coach company, either to a historic city, the races or an attraction? By purchasing admission tickets in bulk and covering the hire of the coach in the ticket price, you can make quite a profit if you sell each ticket for a small profit, as well as create a good social event for your supporters. You can even do a raffle on the coach journey down and sell refreshments and snacks.

Using external businesses

Whilst it is often best to manage your own activities so more of the profit comes directly to your charity, society, club or school, there are numerous ways you can raise funds by using external businesses, from whom you receive a percentage of the money received. Alternatively, think of what you can offer local and national businesses – you might have a large network of supporters, parents or parishioners that a business would be interested in contacting for publicity.

235. Sell advertising space

If you have a weekly, fortnightly, monthly or annual newsletter to a substantial number of supporters, why not sell advertising space to local or national businesses? If it covers the printing of the newsletter alone then this is something! Also consider the advertising space on programmes for your event and other printed items on sale such as calendars.

236. Rent / hire out equipment

If you have specialised equipment such as a disco and lights system or microphone and speakers, rent them out to other organisations for a small charge. A disco unit rented out once a week for £30 would bring in over £1,500 in one year.

237. Rent rooms

If your organisation or charity has a number of vacant rooms at different times of the day, rent them out to other local societies, organisations or groups such as book clubs, art groups, dance classes, after school clubs etc. It is amazing how quickly the money mounts up. If you rent one room out for two days a week for £20 each, then you would raise over £2,000 every year.

238. Rent parking or storage space

If your organisation has a car park that is seldom used or only used at certain times of the day or week, apply for a car parking license from your council and rent out the space during peak shopping times. The same can be said for any clean and secure storage space you have available.

239. School uniform & photo companies

A number of clothing and photo companies will donate a percentage of all orders received by your charity, club, society or school, so ensure the company that is providing your branded sweaters, tops, book bags and school photos partake in a donation scheme.

240. Local companies and reward schemes

Contact local companies to see if they would be interested in running a loyalty scheme with your organisation and supporters. Anything bought by your supporters over a period of time at the shop is recorded (by retaining receipts), with a small percentage of the total amount spent paid back to your organisation once a year. For example, you could contact your local garden centre and everyone who shopped there in one year keeps their receipts, which are then added together and 10% of the total amount is paid back to your charity or school. Not only is it great publicity for the garden centre but it creates customer loyalty as people know they are also helping their local charity or school. If a yearlong campaign is too much, then why not consider campaigns for specific times of the year, for example Christmas? During November and December, why not suggest that for every Christmas tree sold to a parent at your school, 10% of the price will be donated back to the school as part of a loyalty scheme? 100 parents buying a tree for £20 would bring the garden centre £2,000 as well as great publicity and the school would receive £200. Imagine if this scheme was carried on throughout the year, when parents come to the garden centre to buy hanging baskets, spring and summer bulbs, autumn flowers and even garden furniture and barbecues.

241. Sell stalls at events

If you haven't enough volunteers at your event to run all the stalls you would like, then rent out tables and space to outside companies or individuals. Not only does it raise extra cash to go towards your fundraising target but it also creates a bigger draw to your event as more items and activities are on offer to visitors and passers-by. You could either charge an amount per table or ask for people to give a donation of all takings received that day.

242. Contact companies for old stock

This is a great idea once the Boxing day and New Year sales have finished. Companies often have surplus stock they need to shift in order to make way for new products. Managers are often happy to either sell the stock at a huge discount or donate it to a good cause, so it worth asking in person or writing a letter to tell them about your fundraising and what you are raising money for. Remember, if you don't ask, you don't get! The worst anybody can say is 'no!'

243. Company demonstrations

There are many companies that run a demonstration evening of their products, where people will give a free presentation about their products either at someone's house or in a village hall. The person 'hosting' the event (which could be you on behalf of your charity, society, club or school) receives free gifts in return (which you can then sell or donate to future raffles as prizes) as well as a percentage of the total amount purchased through the event. Not only can these events raise considerable sums for your good cause, but they are great social occasions for you, your supporters and potentially new supporters to enjoy. You could also advertise the event locally to encourage more people to attend, as the more people that come, the more money that is likely to be spent and thus raised.

Following are a range of companies (arranged by the type of products they are selling) that offer this type of 'demonstration and reward' scheme:

Food

Cambrian Meat
Chocolates for Chocoholics
ChocoliciousUk

My Secret Kitchen
Strictly Chocolate
The Secret Pantry

Home and garden

Betterware
Jamie Oliver at Home
Pampered Chef
Demarle Ltd
Girlie Gardening
Gold Canyon

Kleeneze
Linen at Home
Partylite UK Ltd
Tomboy Tools
Tupperware

Craft and cards

Cards at your Fingertips
Phoenix Cards
Craft-ED

Creative Memories
Yellow Moon

Clothes

Ann Summers (lingerie)
Captain Tortue UK Ltd
Knitti

Stardust & Dust Ltd
Toys and Clothes Ltd

Handbags, jewellery and accessories

Crystal Café Limited
Frostfire Jewellery
Jo Magdalena

Miglio, Peggy and Minnie
Something Frivolous
Tiempo Watches

Beauty products

Avon Cosmetics Ltd
Body Shop at Home
Conviviality
Elle Pure
Mary Kay Cosmetics (UK) Ltd

O_Pur cosmetics
Oriflame UK Ltd
Pure and Gentle Skincare
Triorganics
Vie at Home Limited

Baby items

Arabella Miller Ltd
Bebeco
Boutique for Babies
Close Parent Limited
Grand Baby Ltd

Lollipop Children's Products Ltd
Mamatoto Ltd
Mini Marmalade
The Keepsake Co
Truly Madly Baby

Toys

Blackberrie Bears
Butterflies and Dragons
Little Living
Mini-IQ LTD

Tish Tash Toys
Toys and Clothes Ltd
Toys to You

Books

Barefoot Books Ltd
Poppy's Books

Usborne Books at Home
Scholastic books

Environmental products

EcoFlow
ENJO UK

Wikaniko Ltd

Using the internet

Following are a selection of ideas on how you can make money or raise your profile on the internet, and consequently gain more supporters locally, nationally and even internationally who can help with your fundraising activities:

244. Get a website

It goes without saying how important the internet is for marketing, spreading awareness and general communication on what you are doing and events being planned, so it is essential that you acquire a professional looking website. However, this doesn't have to be expensive or difficult! Companies such as Mr. Site (www.mrsite.co.uk) offer professional templates for you to use and start at less than £20 a year, including your domain name and email addresses. By having a website, you can keep supporters up to date on activities and events being planned as well as any financial targets you are aiming for. Make sure you utilize your 'meta-tags' fully so that people can find you on search engines such as Google and Yahoo.

245. Website advertising

Once you have your website, make sure you use it to the maximum with linked web advertising, either with Google Ads or by selling advertising space to local and national businesses connected to your aims. You can also offer exchange adverts with another charity or a related society.

246. Internet purchases

Register at www.easyfundraising.org.uk and encourage your supporters to go through this site when buying from their favourite online retailers. It doesn't cost your supporters any extra by doing this, but your charity or school will receive cash back payments up to 15% of whatever has been bought by your supporters, with no catch to you and no catch to the consumer. Why not recommend your supporters have this website as their homepage so they don't forget to just click on it first before they go off and do their online shopping? Also, make sure you promote this at key times of the year – well before Christmas to remind people as well as Mother's Day and Father's Day.

247. Social networking sites

Establish your charity, society, club or school on social networking sites such as Facebook, Twitter and MySpace in order to spread awareness of future events you are planning and fundraising targets you are aiming for. You can link your page to other pages and create a wider local, national and international network of supporters. 'Causes' on Facebook is a popular way for individuals and charities to promote awareness of their campaigns. By setting yourself up and spreading the word among current friends and supporters, you will be amazed how quickly your cause will grow in support, which is fantastic for telling people about your aims, targets and forthcoming events.

248. Write a blog

If you are a keen writer and can write witty, amusing or thought-provoking material then start writing a blog on your website. Not only will you keep your supporters up to date on how the fundraising is going, but by writing on the internet you can start to attract followers from all over the world. Whilst it might not transcend directly into money straight away, a blog is a great way of making the fundraising personal, up to date and interesting.

249. Online auctions and E-bay

You can sell items on an online auction (such as www.mycharityservices.com or EBay) to raise money for your charity, promoting the auction through your supporters on social network sites such as Facebook and Twitter. Alternatively, you can ask supporters who sell items on EBay whether they could add a donation option to every sale. This way people who buy items from these sellers can choose whether they would like to add a donation to their total purchase price, just a small amount so it is hardly noticed by them, say fifty pence. Small amounts such as these accumulated over numerous sales over a period of time can generate a substantial amount for your charity for little or no work whatsoever.

250. Sell books via Amazon Associates

By registering yourself with Amazon Associates, you can sell books via your website through Amazon. You are not handling any of the books or payment transactions yourself, merely redirecting any potential customers to Amazon, from whom you receive a percentage of any sales made. You can list the books you want on your website, consequently making a 'library of recommended books' that is appropriate to your fundraising cause.

251. Create and sell an e-book

If you or your supporters are keen writers, then why not write an e-book and put it on your website for people to download for a small charge? It doesn't cost you anything to do and the majority of the money comes back to you (with just the company processing the payment taking a small percentage such as PayPal). Alternatively, if you are interested in writing a book that raises money for your fundraising cause as well as spread awareness about a particular issue then contact the publishers of this book, Nell James Publishers.

252. Widgets and Apps

Put the WhatGives!? or Chipin on your Facebook page, website, blog, Twitter or I-phone. It displays your fundraising goal, has a donate button and is easy to share amongst all your supporters and for them to circulate it amongst their friends and family members. All donations are handled via PayPal, making it easy to collect the funds raised.

253. Online petitions

If you are looking to create an online petition to create awareness or change a law, then look at one of the following companies (www.petitiononline.com or www.change.org) who create a petition for free and offer advice on circulating it to your supporters and the wider public, thus raising your profile considerably.

***

So there you have it - over 250 fundraising ideas for your charity, society, club or school. If you like this book, then please leave a positive review on Amazon! If you don't like the book, then please send me an email via Nell James Publishers (info@nelljames.co.uk) so that I can improve any subsequent editions. With your help and suggestions, I might even compile 500+ fundraising ideas!

Following are appendices of dates that you can link a fundraising event to – national days, awareness days and historical anniversaries. These can be particularly useful if you are looking for something in a particular month and are seeking inspiration for a theme. Just have a look at the following appendices and you might just find something that is suitable yet different!

Finally, thank you once again for purchasing this book and helping me raise money for the NSPCC (National Society for the Prevention of Cruelty to Children). Good luck with your fundraising efforts and on behalf of all the people, animals and good causes you are helping, thank you!

Paige
x

Appendix A: National days

Following is a list of celebrated national days from across the world (arranged by date), which are an excellent way to create a theme for your event. They can also help you to link your fundraising to the plight of others elsewhere, especially if your charity or society is raising money for an international cause:

January

1 January	Cuba (Liberation Day)
1 January	Haiti (Declaration of Independence from France, 1804)
26 January	Australia (Australia Day)

February

6 February	New Zealand (Waitangi Day, signing of the Treaty of Waitangi, 1840)
11 February	Japan (National Foundation Day, the first Emperor Jimmu is crowned in 660 BC)
24 February	Estonia (Independence from Russia, 1918)

March

1 March	Wales (St. David's Day)
2 March	Morocco (Independence from France, 1956)
17 March	Ireland (St. Patrick's Day)
25 March	Greece (Declaration of Independence from Ottoman Empire, 1821)
26 March	Bangladesh (Declaration of Independence from Pakistan, 1971)

April

18 April	Zimbabwe (Declaration of Independence from the United Kingdom, 1980)
23 April	England (St. George's Day)
25 April	Anzac Day
27 April	South Africa (First democratic general election, 1994)

May

9 May	Guernsey, Jersey, Alderney and dependencies (Liberation Day as end of the German Occupation, 1945)
17 May	Norway (The signing of the first Norwegian Constitution in Eidsvoll, 1814)

June

2 June	Italy (Festa della Repubblica, voted a Republic, 1946; Giuseppe Garibaldi died on this date, 1882)
5 June	Denmark (Constitution of 1849)
6 June	Sweden (Gustav Vasa is elected King of Sweden, 1523)
10 June	Portugal (Portugal Day)
12 June	Russian Federation (Declaration of sovereignty, 1990)
17 June	Iceland (Founding of Republic and dissolution of union with Denmark, 1944)
25 June	Croatia (Declaration of Independence from Yugoslavia, 1991)
26 June	Madagascar (Independence from France, 1960)

July

1 July	Canada (Canada Day)
1 July	Hong Kong (Transfer of sovereignty to the People's Republic of China, 1997)
4 July	United States (Independence Day)
5 July	Isle of Man
9 July	Argentina (Declaration of Independence from Spain, 1816)
10 July	Bahamas (Independence from the United Kingdom, 1973)
11 July	Mongolia (Declaration of Independence from China, 1921)
14 July	France (Fête de la Fédération, 14 July 1790)
21 July	Belgium
23 July	Egypt (Revolution Day, from the Revolution of 1952)
28 July	Peru (Declaration of Independence from Spain, 1821)

August

1 August	Jamaica (Independence from the United Kingdom, 1962)
1 August	Switzerland (National Day)
4 August	Cook Islands (Self-government with New Zealand, 1965)
9 August	Singapore (Separation from Malaysia, 1965)
10 August	Ecuador (Independence from Spain, 1809)
15 August	Republic of India (Independence Day from the British Empire, 1947)
24 August	Ukraine (Independence from the Soviet Union, 1991)

September

2 September	Vietnam (Declaration of Independence from France and Japan, 1945)
7 September	Brazil (Declaration of Independence from Portugal, 1822)
10 September	Gibraltar, United Kingdom (Gibraltar National Day)
15 September	Costa Rica (Independence from Spain, 1821)
16 September	Mexico (Independence from Spain, 1810)
18 September	Chile (The first Government Junta is created, 1810)
21 September	Malta (Independence from the United Kingdom, 1964)
23 September	Saudi Arabia (Unification of the kingdoms, 1932)
30 September	Botswana (Independence from the United Kingdom, 1966)

October

1 October	People's Republic of China (Proclamation, 1949)
1 October	Cyprus (Independence Day, 1960)
1 October	Nigeria (Independence from United Kingdom, 1960)
3 October	Germany (German Unity Day, unification of West Germany and East Germany 1990)
9 October	Uganda (Independence from the United Kingdom, 1962)
10 October	Fiji (Independence from United Kingdom, 1970)
12 October	Spain (Columbus discovery of America, 1492)
26 October	Austria (Neutrality Constitution, 1955)
28 October	Czech Republic (Independence from Austria-Hungary, 1918)
29 October	Turkey (Republican constitution, 1923)

November

1 November	Algeria (Beginning of War of Independence, 1954)
9 November	Cambodia (Independence from France, 1953)
11 November	Poland (Independence Day from Austro-Hungary, Prussia, and Russia, 1918)
30 November	Barbados (Independence from the United Kingdom, 1966)
30 November	Scotland (St. Andrew's Day)

December

2 December	Laos (People's Republic declared, 1975)
5 December	Thailand (Birthday of King Bhumibol Adulyadej)
6 December	Finland (Independence from Russia, 1917)
12 December	Kenya (Independence from the United Kingdom, 1963)
28 December	Nepal (Birthday of the King)

Appendix B: Awareness days

There are special days, weeks and months throughout the world when awareness on a specific issue is highlighted. Why not attach your fundraising to one of these international dates to increase publicity about the work you are doing?

January

4 January	World Braille Day
27 January	Holocaust Memorial Day

February

Lesbian Gay Bisexual Trans History Month
Second week in February is World Orphan Week (SOS)

4 February	World Cancer Day
12 February	Red Hand Day (Against the use of Child Soldiers)
12 February	Darwin Day
15 February	International Childhood Cancer Day
20 February	World Day of Social Justice
21 February	International Mother Language Day

March

Veggie month
Last week in March is Week of Solidarity with the Peoples Struggling against Racism and Racial Discrimination
First Thursday in March is World Book Day
Second Monday in March is Commonwealth Day

1 March	Self-Injury Awareness Day

8 March	International Women's Day (also United Nations Day for Women's Rights and International Peace)
11 March	World Kidney Day
20 March	World Earth Day (as recognised by the United Nations, although some countries celebrate it on 22 April)
21 March	International Day for the Elimination of Racial Discrimination
21 March	World Poetry Day
21 March	World Forestry Day
21 March	World Down Syndrome Day
22 March	World Day for Water
24 March	World Tuberculosis Day
25 March	International Day of Remembrance of the Victims of Slavery and the Transatlantic Slave Trade
27 March	World Theatre Day

April

National Autism Month
National Pet Month
Second week in April is World Homeopathy Awareness Week

2 April	International Children's Book Day
2 April	World Autism Day
6 April	Tartan Day
7 April	World Health Day
11 April	World Parkinsons Day
17 April	World Haemophilia Day
22 April	International Mother Earth Day
23 April	World Book and Copyright Day
25 April	World Malaria Day
28 April	International Workers' Memorial Day
29 April	International Make-A-Wish Day
29 April	International Dance Day

May

Local and Community History Month
National Share-a-Story Month
First week in May is International Youth Week
Mid-May is M.E. Awareness Week
First Tuesday in May is World Asthma Day

3 May	World Press Freedom Day
4 May	International Fire Fighters Day
5 May	International Day of the Midwife
8 May	World Red Cross Day
8 May	World Fair Trade Day
10 May	World Lupus Day
12 May	International Nurses Day
12 May	International Fibromyalgia Awareness Day
15 May	International Day of Families
17 May	International Day Against Homophobia
18 May	International Museums Day
21 May	World Day for Cultural Development
22 May	World Biodiversity Day
25 May	National Missing Children's Day
29 May	International Day of UN Peacekeepers
31 May	World No-Tobacco Day

June

National Vaccination Month
National Osteoporosis Month
Male Cancer Awareness Month
Mid-June is World Diabetes Week
Late-June is Deafblind Awareness Week

1 June	International Children's Day
4 June	International Day of Innocent Children Victims of Aggression
5 June	World Environment Day
8 June	World Oceans Day
12 June	World Day Against Child Labour

14 June	World Blood Donor Day
15 June	World Elder Abuse Awareness Day
16 June	Day of the African Child
17 June	World Day to Combat Desertification and Drought
18 June	Autistic Pride Day
20 June	World Refugee Day
21 June	World Music Day
26 June	International Day against Drug Abuse and Illicit Trafficking
26 June	International Day in Support of Victims of Torture

July

First week July is Deaf Awareness Week

Early July is Transplant Awareness Week

| 11 July | World Population Day |
| 18 July | Nelson Mandela International Day |

August

First week in August is World Breastfeeding Week

Mid-August is World Water Week

9 August	International Day of the World's Indigenous People
12 August	International Youth Day
19 August	World Humanitarian Day
23 August	International Day for the Remembrance of the Slave Trade and Its Abolition
29 August	International Day against Nuclear Tests

September

Childhood Cancer Awareness Month

Thyroid Cancer Awareness Month
First week in September is International Suicide Prevention Awareness Week

8 September	International Literacy Day
10 September	World Suicide Prevention Day
15 September	International Day of Democracy
16 September	International Day for the Preservation of the Ozone Layer
19 September	International Talk Like a Pirate Day
21 September	International Day of Peace
21 September	World Alzheimer Day
22 September	OneWebDay
23 September	World Maritime Day
26 September	World Heart Day
26 September	European Day of Languages
27 September	World Tourism Day

October

Black History Month
Breast Cancer Awareness Month
International School Libraries Month
International Walk to School Month
World Blindness Awareness Month
Last week in October is Disarmament Week
First Monday in October is World Habitat Day
Second Wednesday in October is International Day for Natural Disaster Reduction
Second Thursday in October is World Sight Day

1 October	International Day for Older Persons
1 October	International Music Day
1 October	World Smile Day
2 October	International Day of Non-Violence
4 October	World Animal Day
5 October	International World Teacher's Day
10 October	World Hospice and Palliative Care Day

10 October	World Mental Health Day
12 October	World Arthritis Day
16 October	World Food Day
17 October	International Day for the Eradication of Poverty
22 October	International Stuttering Awareness Day

November

First week in November is National Adoption Week
First week in November is International Brain Tumour Awareness Week

1 November	World Vegan Day
3 November	National Stress Awareness Day
14 November	World Diabetes Day
15 November	International PEN Day of the Imprisoned Writer
16 November	International Day of Tolerance
20 November	Universal Children's Day
21 November	World Hello Day
21 November	World Television Day
25 November	International Day for the Elimination of Violence against Women

December

1 December	World Aids Day
2 December	International Day for the Abolition of Slavery
3 December	International Day for Disabled Persons
5 December	International Volunteer Day
10 December	International Human Rights Day
20 December	International Human Solidarity Day

Appendix C: Historical dates

There are many historical dates throughout the year that you could use for your event. For example, if your fundraising is for human rights, then why not stage it on 11 February, the day Nelson Mandela was released from prison, or hold a concert on the anniversary of Live Aid (13 July)? Or if your event is to support women, consider holding it on 6 August, the date the first woman ever swam the English Channel.

Following are a selection of key historical and cultural anniversaries alongside some famous birthdays that you could link your fundraising event to:

January

1 January	The immigration station on Ellis Island, New York Harbour, opened (1892)
4 January	Isaac Newton born (1643)
5 January	Twelfth Night
8 January	George Washington delivered the first ever *State of the Union* address (1790)
8 January	Elvis Presley born (1935)
12 January	The National Trust is established in Britain (1895)
12 January	Haiti earthquake (2010)
15 January	Martin Luther King born (1929)
20 January	John F. Kennedy's inaugural speech: 'ask not what your country can do for you — ask what you can do for your country' (1961)
20 January	Barack Obama was inaugurated as the first African American President of the United States (2009)
21 January	Concorde began supersonic commercial flights (1976)

25 January	Nellie Bly, American journalist, completed a circumnavigation of the globe in a then record 72 days (1890)
27 January	Lewis Carroll born (1832)
27 January	The liberation of Auschwitz (1945)
29 January	Queen Victoria created the Victoria Cross, in recognition of the acts of bravery by soldiers during the Crimean War (1856)
30 January	Mohandas Karamchand Gandhi was fatally shot in Delhi (1948)

February

1 February	Harriet Tubman is the first black woman honoured on a US postage stamp (1978)
1 February	First volume of the *Oxford English Dictionary* published (1884)
2 February	Groundhog Day
2 February	Alexander Selkirk is rescued from a shipwreck on a desert island, inspiring the book *Robinson Crusoe* by Daniel Defoe (1709)
4 February	Rosa Parks, civil rights activist, born (1913)
7 February	The classic board game *Monopoly* is invented (1935)
9 February	The Davis Cup competition is established (1900)
10 February	Queen Victoria of the United Kingdom marries Prince Albert of Saxe-Coburg-Gotha (1840)
11 February	Thomas Alva Edison born (1847)
11 February	After 27 years as a political prisoner, Nelson Mandela released from Victor Verster Prison, South Africa (1990)
12 February	Charles Darwin born (1809)
12 February	Anna Pavlova, Russian ballerina, born (1881)
15 February	Galileo Galilei born (1564)

15 February	Great Ormond St Hospital for Sick Children, London admits its first patient (1852)
16 February	Kyoto Protocol on climate change came into force (2005)
22 February	George Washington, First President of the United States, born (1732)
23 February	Richard Palmer is identified as the outlaw Dick Turpin at York Castle (1739)
24 February	The first parade to have floats is staged at Mardi Gras in New Orleans, Louisiana (1868)

March

1 March	Yellowstone National Park (US) is established as the world's first national park (1872)
3 March	Steve Fossett becomes the first person to fly an airplane non-stop around the world solo without refuelling (2005)
3 March	Alexander Graham Bell, Scottish-Canadian inventor, born (1847)
4 March	John Flamsteed is appointed the first Astronomer Royal of England (1675)
6 March	Michelangelo, Italian artist and sculptor, born (1475)
9 March	The Barbie doll makes its debut at the American International Toy Fair in New York (1959)
14 March	Albert Einstein born (1879)
15 March	United Nations Human Rights Council established (2006)
15 March	Julius Caesar, Dictator of the Roman Republic, is stabbed to death by Marcus Junius Brutus, and several other Roman senators on the Ides of March (44 BC)
16 March	Wanderers F.C. wins the first FA Cup, oldest football competition in the world (1872)

18 March	Aleksei Leonov becomes the first person to walk in space (1965)
23 March	Patrick Henry's 'Give me Liberty, or give me Death!' speech to the Virginia House of Burgesses (1775)
25 March	Robert the Bruce becomes King of Scotland, crowned two days later at Scone (1306)
25 March	The Slave Trade Act ('An Act for the Abolition of the Slave Trade') was passed in Britain (1807)
30 March	Vincent van Gogh born (1853)
31 March	Johann Sebastian Bach born (1685)

April

1 April	April Fool's Day
4 April	The Beatles occupy the top five positions on the US Billboard Hot 100 pop chart (1964)
4 April	Martin Luther King, Jr. is assassinated by James Earl Ray in Tennessee (1968)
7 April	William Wordsworth born (1770)
8 April	Siddhartha Gautama born, the founder of Buddhism (563 BC)
10 April	The Titanic leaves port in Southampton, England for her first and only voyage (1912)
11 April	Charles Hallé, German pianist and conductor, born (1819)
14 April	Tiananmen Square Protests began (1989)
15 April	RMS Titanic sank (1912)
15 April	Hillsborough disaster (1989)
19 April	Captain James Cook sights the eastern coast of Australia (1770)
22 April	Sir Robin Knox-Johnston completes the first solo non-stop circumnavigation of the world (1969)
23 April	William Shakespeare died (1616)

25 April	Anzac Day
26 April	William Shakespeare baptised (1564)
27 April	Betty Boothroyd becomes the first woman in its 700-year history to be elected Speaker of the British House of Commons (1992)
29 April	World Wide Fund for Nature was established (1961)

May

1 May	Calamity Jane, American Wild West performer, born (1852)
1 May	The 1940 Summer Olympics are cancelled due to the Second World War (1940)
2 May	*Good Housekeeping* magazine begins (1885)
3 May	Festival of Britain opens (1951)
4 May	Audrey Hepburn born (1929)
6 May	Roger Bannister becomes the first person to run the mile in under four minutes (1954)
8 May	Jean Henri Dunant, Founder of the Red Cross, born (1828)
8 May	Victory in Europe day (VE Day) after the Second World War (1945)
10 May	Bill Haley & His Comets release *Rock Around the Clock*, the first rock and roll record to reach number one (1954)
10 May	Nelson Mandela is inaugurated as South Africa's first black president (1994)
12 May	Florence Nightingale born (1820)
14 May	The NSPCC is launched in London (1889)
20 May	Amelia Earhart starts her flight to become the first woman to fly solo non-stop across the Atlantic (1932)
23rd May	*Treasure Island* by Robert Louis Stevenson published (1883)
24 May	First Eurovision Song Contest is held (1956)

26 May	Miles Davis born (1926)
29 May	John F. Kennedy born (1917)
29 May	Edmund Hillary and Tenzing Norgay reach the summit of Mount Everest (1953)
29 May	'Ain't I A Woman?' speech delivered at the Women's Convention in Akron, Ohio by Sojourner Truth, a former slave in New York State (1851)

June

1 June	Marilyn Monroe born (1926)
2 June	Thomas Hardy born
4 June	The first Pulitzer Prizes are awarded (1917)
4 June	'We Shall Fight On The Beaches' speech delivered by Winston Churchill to the British parliament (1940)
10 June	First boat race between Oxford University and Cambridge University (1829)
10 June	Judy Garland born (1922)
10 June	Alcoholics Anonymous is founded (1935)
12 June	Anne Frank born (1929) and receives a diary for her thirteenth birthday (1942)
14 June	The Stars and Stripes Flag is adopted by the United States (1777)
14 June	Mutiny on the Bounty survivors reach Timor after a 4,000-mile journey in an open boat (1789)
16 June	Valentina Tereshkova (Russian astronaut) became the first woman to fly in space (1963)
16 June	RSPCA founded as the Society for the Prevention of Cruelty to Animals (1824)
19 June	Aung San Suu Kyi (Burmese politician and peace activist) born (1945)
20 June	Queen Victoria succeeds to the British throne (1837)

25 June	*The Diary of a Young Girl* (better known as *The Diary of Anne Frank*) is published (1947)
30 June	Charles Blondin crosses Niagara Falls on a tightrope (1859)
30 June	First Harry Potter book published, *Harry Potter and the Philosopher's Stone* (1997)

July

1 July	The first Gay Pride march in England takes place (1972)
1 July	Sony introduces the Walkman (1979)
2 July	Steve Fossett becomes the first person to fly solo around the world nonstop in a balloon (2002)
3 July	The Representation of the People (Equal Franchise) Act became law in the UK, granting women the same voting rights as men (1928)
4 July	*Alice's Adventures in Wonderland* is published (1865)
5 July	The Salvation Army is founded (1865)
6 July	Tenzin Gyatso, the 14th Dalai Lama, born (1935)
7 July	Boris Becker becomes the youngest player ever to win Wimbledon at age 17 (1985)
11 July	*A Tale of Two Cities* by Charles Dickens is published (1859)
11 July	*To Kill a Mockingbird* by Harper Lee is first published (1960)
13 July	Live Aid (1985)
14 July	Bastille Day (1789)
14 July	Emmeline Pankhurst, English suffragette, born (1858)
18 July	Nelson Mandela born (1918)

21 July	Neil Armstrong and Edwin 'Buzz' Aldrin become the first men to walk on the Moon (1969)
24 July	Amelia Earhart, American aviator, born (1897)
25 July	Louise Brown, the world's first 'test tube baby' is born (1978)
26 July	Wolfgang Amadeus Mozart born (1791)
28 July	Beatrix Potter born (1866)
31 July	J. K. Rowling born (1965)

August

1 August	Slavery was officially abolished in most of the British Empire (1834)
6 August	Gertrude Caroline Ederle became the first woman to swim the English Channel (1926)
6 August	Hiroshima in Japan became the first city in history to be destroyed by a nuclear weapon (1945)
9 August	Johann Michael Bach born (1648)
9 August	Second atomic bomb dropped on Nagasaki in Japan by the USA, during the Second World War (1945)
11 August	Babe Ruth becomes the first baseball player to hit 500 home runs in his career (1929)
15 August	Victory over Japan Day as Japan surrenders, Second World War (1945)
15 August	The Woodstock Music and Art Festival begins (1969)
20 August	'Never was so much owed by so many to so few' speech by Winston Churchill was broadcast on the radio (1940)
22 August	St. Columba reports seeing a monster in Loch Ness, Scotland (565)
24 August	Captain Matthew Webb became first person to swim the English Channel (1875)

26 August   Mother Teresa born (1910)
28 August   Martin Luther King gave his 'I have a dream' speech (1963)

September

1 September	Terry Fox's *Marathon of Hope* ends in Thunder Bay, Ontario (1980)
2 September	The Great Fire of London starts (1666)
4 September	Google is founded (1998)
6 September	Jan Addams, US pioneer in women rights and peace, born (1860)
7 September	Buddy Holly born (1936)
11 September	First British Women's Institute meeting (1915)
11 September	Foundation of the World Wildlife Fund (1961)
11 September	The September 11 attacks take place in the United States (2001)
13 September	Roald Dahl born (1916)
15 September	Agatha Christie born (1890)
15 September	Battle of Britain Day
18 September	The Blackpool Illuminations are switched on for the first time (1879)
18 September	The first official Paralympic Games held in Rome (1960)
18 September	Joe Kittinger completes the first solo balloon crossing of the Atlantic (1984)
19 September	Sir William Golding born (1911)
19 September	The first Glastonbury Festival held (1970)
20 September	The first Cannes Film Festival is held (1946)
21 September	J. R. R. Tolkien's *The Hobbit* is published (1937)
23 September	Neptune is discovered (1846)
24 September	Sir Arthur Guinness, Irish brewer of the famous Guinness drink, born (1725)
26 September	T. S. Eliot born (1888)
28 September	Penicillin discovered (1928)

October

1 October	Mensa is founded in the United Kingdom (1946)
1 October	NASA is created (1958)
2 October	Mohandas Karamchand Gandhi born (1869)
2 October	*Peanuts* by Charles M. Schulz is first published (1950)
4 October	First run of the Orient Express (1883)
4 October	First Boys' Brigade meeting (1883)
5 October	*Dr. No*, the first in the James Bond film series, is released (1962)
5 October	The Beatles release their first single, *Love Me Do* (1962)
6 October	Thomas Edison shows his first motion picture (1889)
6 October	Jason Lewis completes the first human-powered circumnavigation of the globe (2007)
7 October	Desmond Tutu born (1931)
9 October	John Lennon born (1940)
9 October	The musical *The Phantom of the Opera* has its first performance (1986)
9 October	Human Rights Act in the UK (1998)
14 October	*Winnie-the-Pooh* by A.A. Milne is first published (1926)
25 October	Pablo Picasso born (1881)

November

4 November	Barack Obama becomes the first African-American to be elected President of the United States (2008)
5 November	Gunpowder Plot or Guy Fawkes Night (1605)
7 November	Captain James Cook born (1728)
7 November	Marie Curie born (1867)
9 November	Berlin Wall comes down (1989)

11 November	Armistice signed ending the First World War (1918)
19 November	Football player Pelé scores his 1,000th goal (1969)
22 November	The Humane Society of the United States is founded (1954)
23 November	The first jukebox used, at the Palais Royale Saloon in San Francisco (1889)
24 November	Charles Darwin publishes *On the Origin of Species* (1859)
25 November	*The Mousetrap* opens at the Ambassadors Theatre in London later becoming the longest continuously-running play in history (1952)
27 November	First Macy's Thanksgiving Day Parade is held (1924)
29 November	Sir John Ambrose Fleming born (1849)
30 November	Mark Twain born (1835)
30 November	The steam locomotive *Flying Scotsman* becomes the first to officially exceed 100mph (1934)

December

1 December	Rosa Parks refuses to give up her bus seat to a white man which leads to the Montgomery Bus Boycott (1955)
5 December	James Christie holds his first auction (1766)
5 December	Walt Disney born (1901)
6 December	The first edition of the *Encyclopædia Britannica* is published (1768)
6 December	The Thirteenth Amendment to the United States Constitution was adopted in the US, officially abolishing and continuing to prohibit slavery and involuntary servitude (1865)
7 December	The Royal Opera House opens at Covent Garden, London (1732)
7 December	Attack on Pearl Harbour (1941)

10 December	The first Nobel Prizes are awarded (1901)
12 December	Frank Sinatra born (1915)
15 December	*Gone with the Wind* premières (1939)
17 December	Ludvig van Beethoven baptised (1770)
21 December	The Mayflower Pilgrims land in America (1620)
21 December	Rebecca West, author, born (1892)
21 December	The first crossword puzzle is published in the *New York World* (1913)
21 December	*Snow White and the Seven Dwarfs*, the first full-length animated film, premieres (1937)
21 December	Civil partnerships allowed in England and Wales (2005)
28 December	The Peak District becomes the United Kingdom's first National Park (1950)
30 December	Rudyard Kipling born (1865)

Useful websites

Following are a selection of websites that can offer advice for charities, societies, clubs, individuals and schools regarding fundraising. If any of the websites listed close down or are no longer relevant, or you come across new and better websites that should be added, then please email Nell James Publishers at info@nelljames.co.uk so that the resource section in any further editions of this book can be updated. Additionally, if you have any fundraising ideas you would like to see included in a subsequent edition of this book, then please do email the publishers with your suggestions. With your help we could put together a book containing 500+ fundraising ideas!

(Please note that the author and Nell James Publishers take **no responsibility** for the information and advice contained in the websites listed below and by including the websites in this book the author and publisher are in **no way endorsing** the advice, services and goods on offer.)

General fundraising websites

www.ideasfundraising.co.uk
www.sofii.org/
www.better-fundraising-ideas.com
www.50fundraisingideas.com
www.raisingfunding.co.uk
www.doitforcharity.com
www.worldwidevolunteering.org.uk/FundraisingAdvice.asp
www.redhotfundraisingideas.com
www.crowdrise.com

Gift aid advice

www.hmrc.gov.uk/charities
www.hmrc.gov.uk/individuals/giving/gift-aid.htm
www.giftaidhelp.org

Financial, legal, & management advice

www.charitycommission.gov.uk
www.cafonline.org
www.institute-of-fundraising.org.uk
www.fundraising.co.uk
www.raisingfunding.co.uk/legal-advice-on-fundraising.html
www.lawworks.org.uk
www.redhotfundraisingideas.com
http://managementhelp.org/fndrsng/np_raise/np_raise.htm
www.cranfieldtrust.org
www.mediatrust.org
www.trusteelearning.org
www.reach-online.org.uk
www.willaid.org.uk

Online donations

www.justgiving.com
http://uk.virginmoneygiving.com
www.charitychoice.co.uk
www.donation4charity.org
www.bmycharity.com
www.charitiestrust.org
www. gofundraise.com.au (Australia)
www.yourcause.com
www.mycharityservices.com
www.whatgives.com
www.chipin.com
www.crowdrise.com

Payroll donations

www.apgo.org.uk
www.payrollgivingcentre.org.uk
www.hmrc.gov.uk/businesses/giving/payroll-giving.htm
www.cafonline.org/default.aspx?page=7026
www.bellfundraising.co.uk
www.allaboutgiving.org

Sample sponsorship forms

http://office.microsoft.com/en-us/templates/sponsorship-form-TC030000468.aspx
www.g-nation.co.uk/teachers/downloads/docs/   SponsorshipForm.doc

Online petition form

www.change.org – online petition
www.petitiononline.com – online petition
http://petitions.number10.gov.uk/
www.petitionspot.com
www.gopetition.co.uk

Free clip art

www.free-graphics.com
www.1clipart.com
www.free-clipart-pictures.net
www.clipartcastle.com
www.dorlingkindersley-uk.co.uk/static/cs/uk/11/clipart/
www.hasslefreeclipart.com
www.aaaclipart.com
www.clipart.co.uk
www.allfreeclipart.com

Recycling advice

www.recycle4charity.co.uk
www.eachonecounts.co.uk
www.cashforcartridges.co.uk
www.alupro.org.uk/cash-for-your-cans.html
www.recyclingforcash.co.uk
www.recyclingappeal.com

Online shopping rewards

www.easyfundraising.org.uk
www.froggybank.co.uk
www.cashback-rewards.co.uk
www.everyclick.com

Free services for charities

www.goodwillgallery.com/freecharityservices.htm
www.charitiesdirectory.com
www.itforcharities.co.uk
http://sectorspace.org.uk/
www.cafonline.org
www.contributions.org.uk

Free goods for charities

www.goodwillgallery.com/freecharitygoods.htm
www.Bag2school.com
www.itforcharities.co.uk
www.ctxchange.org
www.freeukstuff.com
www.uk.freecycle.org
www.greengonzo.com
www.charityfreebies.co.uk

Index